MW00592804

ADMIT ONE

SPECIAL CODE:
MAKEYOURMARKNOW

FOR PURCHASING THIS BOOK, YOU ARE ENTITLED ACCESS TO THE

MAKE YOUR MARK
MASTER COURSE

featuring 14 custom video modules and activity sheets from the author that correspond with this book

Visit the book's website and enter the code above to gain access.

www.TheMakeYourMarkBook.com

Get out today and make your mark on the world!

PRAISE FOR
MAKE YOUR MARK

"Achieving the pinnacles of success never results from one giant leap. Instead, it is the constant and consistent trail of small steps that slowly, but surely, gets you there. This book lays out a clear path to establish a solid vision and understand what it takes to get you there."

Dr. Nido Qubein, President of High Point University, author, hall of fame speaker, Chairman of Great Harvest Company

"What's it worth to you to actually find out how your life can be if you refuse to settle for the status quo? Where would you end up if you truly chased your passions in life? Believe me, the reality can actually surpass the dream. This book *Make Your Mark*, is a road map, a GPS, to help you get to your destination!"

Jim Miller, 10x NCAA Championship Coach, Wartburg College

"Success is something you must pursue if you want to bring it to fruition. In *Make Your Mark*, Dr. Cooper outlines the specific steps you can take that will help you create habits that allow you to achieve your highest aspirations."

Cindy Miller, former LPGA player, NCAA Division I All-American, speaker and corporate trainer

"Finally a book written with the audacity to challenge us not to waste our lives, but to live intentionally, leaving our mark on the earth. It provides a blueprint to live purposefully, while reminding us to PURSUE THE THINGS we're MEANT TO DO while there's still time. A must read. Coyte Cooper helps redefine the true meaning of legacy."

Manny Ohonme, Founder, President, and CEO of Samaritan's Feet, author of *Sole Purpose*, international speaker

"We all want success in our lives. In *Make Your Mark*, Coyte Cooper provides not only a playbook for that success but also gives a voice to the person inside us all trying to break through. It is a must read for every educator, reminding us all of the impact we are capable of having if we unlock the potential Coyte inspires us to reach for."

Brent Wise, Award winning educator, Director of Hilliard Innovative Learning Center

"Dr. Cooper's burning desire to win and uncanny level of discipline has launched him into his destiny as a full-time author, life coach, and speaker. He will be known as one of the top motivators in the world for groups of people who want to achieve greatness and make their mark in this world!"

Josh Liske, World champion, author, international speaker, CEO, www.JoshLiske.com

"Coyte nails it with *Make Your Mark*. Ever since I was little, I always believed that one day I was going to do something special, even though those around me told me that wouldn't be the case. Well, today, I am the founder & CEO of one of the largest employment agencies in the United States and I was awarded the Ernst & Young Entrepreneur of the Year. I urge you to get on the train, read this book, and start your pursuit towards greatness today!"

Aaron Grossman, Chief Executive Officer (CEO), Alliance Solutions Group, LLC

"Far too many people live their life without energy and purpose. Dr. Cooper's *Make Your Mark* book will inspire you with the passion to live with intention and leave a legacy."

Jon Gordon, *New York Times* bstselling author, *The Energy Bus* and *The Carpenter*

"Most of our lives we have been encouraged by teachers and mentors to dream big. In *Make Your Mark*, Dr. Cooper takes this concept a step further and actually provides a road map to success and living out those big dreams. The changes that this book have brought to my life are incredible. Dr. Cooper has helped me realize the importance of setting meaningful goals, developing a growth system that includes the right daily habits, as well as the importance of positivity and the favorable outcomes that are produced when we flip the script on negative thoughts. *Make Your Mark* was written for anyone who wishes to live an extraordinary life and is a great reminder of what it takes to be a high performer."

Sam Ferguson, Athletic Director, McMurray University

"If you want to be truly extraordinary at something, then you must get up every single day committed to excellence. In *Make Your Mark*, Dr. Cooper outlines an impactful step-by-step process that will allow you to do this so you can achieve your highest aspirations."

Anson Dorrance, 21x NCAA Championship Coach, University of North Carolina Women's Soccer

MAKE YOUR MARK

Remarkable lives are not an accident.
They are earned. Here's how.

COYTE G. COOPER, PH.D.

CONTACT DR. COOPER

To book Dr. Cooper for your event, contact
coytecooper@gmail.com

For more information, go to
www.coytecooper.com

Cover design and interior design by Jennifer Deese
Manufactured in the United States of America

For more information, please contact:

Coyte Cooper Enterprises
www.coytecooper.com
coytecooper@gmail.com

Paperback:
ISBN 13: 978-0-9905636-3-1
ISBN 10: 0-9905636-3-4

To my incredible parents, Gene and Lisa,
who constantly encouraged me to go for it
and always put me first. Your love and support
has given me the opportunity to pursue my dreams
and to make my mark on the world.

AUTHOR'S NOTE

As an author, the coolest thing you can possibly do is to write books that will change people's lives in some way forever. If you work hard enough, you increase the chances of being able to step into reader's lives and change the way that they see things.

Honestly, I am not sure I have always approached writing this way in the past. As I worked on my first book *Impressions*, there was a large chunk of the writing that was about me and realizing my goal of publishing a book. Then I released it and saw the impact that it had on readers.

It humbled me to get messages from readers saying that my book had helped them get through a tough time in their life; a divorce, being fired from a job, or the loss of a loved one. It made me smile each time I received feedback from a reader saying the book had motivated them to pursue their dreams. Each of these meant a lot to me and they inspired me to become a better human being.

As I started *Make Your Mark*, I promised myself that I would always remember the potential to impact lives forever as I sat down to write each day. I tried to remind myself to eliminate my ego so I could write something that would be truly meaningful for readers. I hope you can feel this while reading the book. If it takes you even one step closer to living a life that you truly love, then I will have done my job.

In closing, I want to tell you a little about the cover of the book. As we put together concepts, we posted it on social media to get some feedback from followers. While we were already using a wax seal, one suggested that we use a finger print and added that this was the way that fisherman used to sign their contracts. I was immediately drawn to this idea because my dad, who is one of my heroes, was a commercial fisherman for 25 years in Alaska and I had spent time fishing on his boat. It just made sense.

You see, the wax seal is not only about the connection to my family. It is also symbolic of me signing off on all the work that went in to putting this book together. I truly hope that I did enough to help you realize your dreams so you can eventually sign off on the unique mark that you make on the world!

Sincerely,
Coyte

TABLE OF CONTENTS

S INEVITABLE. PURSUE THE THING YOU ARE MEANT TO DO ALL OUT AND MAKING YOUR MARK IS INEVITABLE. PURSU

Introduction

What Is The Make Your Mark Mindset?

> Life is not easy for any of us, but what of that? We must
> have perseverance and above all confidence in ourselves.
> We must believe we are gifted for something and
> that this thing must be attained.
> - Marie Curie

It's **6:30** in the morning and your alarm has just served notice that it is again time to get your butt up and start the day. Your current favorite tune, the one you felt confident would make it easier to embrace your dreaded mornings, gets gradually louder from your mobile device, but that makes little difference as you automatically hit the snooze button. "It is just too dang early," you tell yourself. Yes, an extra 15 minutes of sleep is just what you need to ensure that the rest of your day is manageable. Just as you escape reality back into a comfy deep sleep, that dang song yanks you back to reality and provides a sobering reminder that you must get up now or there will be consequences. This threat is enough to force you to muster enough energy to wrestle yourself to a hunched position where you make one last attempt to convince your semi-conscious mind that it would be all right to sleep just 10 more minutes. Barely fending off this urge, you drag yourself into the bathroom where you jump into the shower. Wait, maybe jump is too strong of a word here given your current state of mind. Let's use crawl instead. Yep, you crawl into the shower where the warm, soothing water brings your body and mind back to life. It seems that things are starting to look up for you.

Wait, where were we again? Oh yes, the shower part. This brings another dilemma because the water is really comfortable and you don't want to get out. After all, this would mean that you have to officially start the day and this is not something you are quite ready to accept. So, you spend 10 minutes too long in the shower and then have to rush downstairs to grab an instant, "express breakfast" before rushing out the door hoping that traffic will cooperate so you can get to your meeting on time. This is not the way that you wanted to start your day. You have defaulted to a stressed state and the rest of your day pretty much goes accordingly. While there are ups and downs, the consistent theme is that you are looking forward to the end of your day when you can just go home and relax on your couch. The weekend cannot come soon enough! Heck, your vacation six months from now can't come soon enough!

I know what some of you are thinking. This situation is NOT representative of my life. Before you get too defensive, consider the fact that the previous example is simply a metaphor symbolic of the general approach that most people have when living their lives. It is entirely possible that you are content with many elements of your life. This is an ideal time to urge you to strongly contemplate the difference between a life that is content and one that is inspired. What exactly would this look like for you if you were brave enough to pursue all your highest aspirations? The fact that you picked up this book tells me that you intuitively know the difference, and that you are not completely charged by the way you are currently living your life. You know deep down that you could be living a far more rewarding life. The good news is that you are not alone. In fact, research has shown that nearly 87 percent of all people are living mundane lives because they have not taken the time to pursue something they are truly passionate about.

Make a Movie About Your Life

Want to know a highly effective strategy to assess your true feelings about the way you are currently living your life? Of course you do! Imagine that your life has been made into a movie that is going to be released for everyone to watch in homes and theatres across the world. It will be a movie that encompasses all of your highest virtues (or lack thereof) as a person and features your key accomplishments up to this point in your life. The way you approach each day, the relationships you have built, and the impact you have made on people will all be front and center for the world to see. Take a moment and close your eyes to envision how you see this movie playing out as of this exact moment in your life. Now stop and ask yourself a simple, yet highly profound question. Are you truly happy with your movie? If you are anything like me, then your initial response is probably not exactly one you would like to openly admit. The verdict is in and you are starring in a movie that is "rotten" on the Tomatometer.

> "87 percent of people never reach their peak performance level because they lack passion for a specific purpose.
> - @coytecooper

Be the Star in a Fresh Film

Let's backtrack a little on the whole "rotten" thing. At first glance, it would seem to indicate that you are starring in a movie that is so terribly bad that nobody would ever want to see it. This is likely not the case at all. Allow me to explain here. On the site RottenTomatoes. com, they have an established Tomatometer that essentially provides a critic rating system for all the movies featured on their site. When a movie is rated positively less than 60 percent of the time, it is given the status of being "rotten" because it is not seen as being a high quality movie worthy of consumer's time. As you reflect on the "flick" created about your life, it is likely that you will come to the conclusion that you have cast yourself as the main character in a mundane movie because you are not living near your full potential. It is not that bad, but it is also not great. Likely around the 59 percent mark where you are hovering between "rotten" and "fresh" on the Tomatometer.

This movie exercise is not being presented to put a dent in your self-confidence. Instead, it is designed to get you to consider the exact type of movie you want to star in so you can make immediate changes in your life to bring it to fruition. I encourage you to really set the type of standards that will allow you to create a flick that is "fresh" and receives acclaim. Sure, your movie might be decent now, but have you done enough to make it so memorable that it earns blockbuster status? Or, if you are currently living well, are you making the type of daily impact that would allow your film to be deserving of an Academy Award? Regardless of your assessment here, the good news is that your movie is not over. There is still time to manifest a plot that will earn you "fresh" status in the future. The key is to determine exactly what type of movie you would like to star in because the strength of your vision will directly mirror the life you experience in the future.

PURSUE PASSION IN YOUR PLOT

Remember that research on the lack of passion that people

have for anything specific in their life? This would mean that nearly 90 percent of all movies made about people would lack any real kind of inspiration that moves audiences. This sounds "rotten" to me! In real life, this equates to about 10 percent of the normal population living with the type of passion that makes a meaningful difference in the world. I don't know about you, but I want to make sure I do everything in my power to be in the "fresh" Tomatometer category when the movie of my life is released. If this resonates with you, then take immediate action to ensure that passion is a central part of your movie's plot. This is what it will take for you to create the type of life that will make a lasting impression on the world. There is nothing mundane about a life where you pursue your full potential in areas that you are passionate about. This will ensure that you star in a movie that is far better than the status quo.

STRIVE FOR MORE THAN THE STATUS QUO

Have you ever asked a person how he or she was doing? Of course you have! If you had not, we would have to assume that there is something wrong with you. Do you know what is equally wrong? The canned response that you get from most people when they answer your question. I bet you can guess the most common response. Ding, ding, ding...we have a winner! It is "I'm fine" or a number of variations that essentially mean the same thing. "So, what's the big deal?" you ask. Seems pretty harmless on the surface. The reason why this is such a big deal is because fine is pretty much a standard response for a boring life where you have settled for the status quo. It is an average approach that will inevitably result in average outcomes. In the movie world, this is the equivalent of a "rotten" status that causes people to avoid your movie.

The reality is that there is nothing challenging and/or exciting about living a life that is just fine. Unfortunately, this has become the norm in our society and the end result is millions of mundane lives that lack passion and energy. We are not going to focus on this route anymore because this book is about taking a proactive approach to transforming your life into something far more meaningful. The good news is that you can absolutely do something to drastically change the main plot of your movie in a reasonable amount of time. While it may sound crazy to you now, I believe that you can inject real energy into your life within a month's time if you commit to implementing the concepts presented in this book. If you cultivate the discipline to turn these behaviors into world-class habits, the end result will be remarkable accomplishments and a life far more rewarding than you ever imagined possible.

What is the "Make Your Mark" Mindset?

It sounds pretty intriguing to hear that you can create a life far more meaningful and productive than the one you are currently living, right? While you may be skeptical, this is absolutely not a gimmick. You will find this to be emphatically true if you choose to fully embrace the "Make Your Mark Mindset" in all areas of your life. What exactly is this mindset? Let's start with a basic definition first. This philosophy is all about developing a mental approach where you are truly passionate about living life at your highest level. It is about cultivating a mindset where you shun the status quo and instead choose to set standards that make everything about you unique. There are no excuses with the "Make Your Mark Mindset" approach. Instead, you take complete responsibility for your current situation and commit to a lifestyle that will allow you to make lasting impressions on the people around you on a daily basis. The end result of this differentiated approach is living so well that people around you pause and wonder how you are able to operate at such an impressive level. This is the same exact philosophy that was embraced by the brilliant entrepreneur Walt Disney when he explained, "What ever you do, do it well. Do it so well that when people see you do it they will want to come back and see you do it again and they will want to bring others and show them how well you do what you do." This mindset is about cultivating a deep inner desire to make your mark on the world. In many ways, it is a legacy move that will ensure that you are remembered far beyond your time on earth. While this alone should inspire you to embrace this mindset, it is important to point out that there are unique benefits to individuals who approach life with this type of passion to live at a high level. Prior to outlining these benefits, let's touch on what this mindset is not so you can be aware of what to avoid in your approach moving forward.

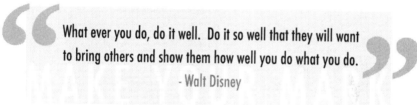

> What ever you do, do it well. Do it so well that they will want to bring others and show them how well you do what you do.
> - Walt Disney

It's Not an Exclusive Club

The Yellowstone Club, located in Big Sky, Montana, was named one of the most prestigious clubs in the United States by Fortune Magazine. Housed on a 13,600-acre private ski and golf course, it is reported that it costs $250,000 to join and has annual dues around $20,000. On top of this, you must also own a home and the average costs here range from $1.65 million for a home site to $18 million for a ranch. This is very much an exclusive club that is reserved for people that are of an elite financial status. When it comes to the "Make Your Mark Mindset," this is not the case at all. It is not an exclusive club that is reserved for any specific segment of the population. It is open to any individual who is determined to pursue their passion and live their best life. However, there is an entry fee that is required for admittance to this lifestyle and that is a willingness to jump way out of your comfort zone regularly embracing doing "little things" that most people are not willing to do. Don't allow yourself to make the mistake of looking at others who are experiencing success and assume they are a part of some special club. The truth is that you can achieve remarkable things by simply practicing the right fundamentals on a daily basis. The question you must ask yourself is, "are you willing to pay the entry fee required to achieve success and make your mark on the world?"

It's Not the Power Ball

Every single year, over 32 million people play the lottery each week in the United Kingdom in hopes of striking it rich. These numbers are staggering and are guaranteed to be much higher in the United States. The fascinating thing is that people spend money on these games on a regular basis with literally no chance of winning. The reason? We have been programmed by our society to want things to come easily and quickly. We dream of striking it rich and having our lives transform into something extravagant and luxurious in an instant. Just imagine what it would be like to never have to worry about bills again. And all of this would come to fruition without you having to even lift a finger. Can you picture it? Now snap out of it because meaningful accomplishments are nothing like the Power Ball! You do yourself a massive disservice if you expect success to appear magically with little to no effort on your part. The same can be said if you hope to lean on luck to achieve your aspirations. You may not realize it now, but this is actually a good thing because success is something you can control through your daily decisions. It is earned when you stop dreaming about winning the Power Ball and instead commit to a lifestyle where you embrace sacrifice and daily doses of excellence.

It's Not a Quantum Leap

While success can deceptively look like it comes quickly and easily for some folks, the truth is that people who have achieved extraordinary levels of success have sacrificed to earn their accomplishments. The part that is deceiving for people observing these high performance individuals is that they are not around when these individuals wake up at 5:00am to invest in developing their skill sets. They do not see the high levels of failure that these people had to overcome to rise to the pinnacle of their respective field. They don't get the chance to observe these successful individuals investing every single day over long periods of time to earn their accomplishments. If you were to study these unique people to inquire about their path to success, they would inevitably tell you about all the sacrifices they had to make to arrive at their current situation in life. It would quickly become apparent that there was no quantum leap that allowed them to become a success story overnight. The process outlined in this book is very much the same. There are no short cuts, but there are routes that you can take to put yourself on a more efficient path to achieve unique accomplishments and meaningful success.

What's In It For You?

It is only natural for you to wonder what is in it for you if you commit to embracing the "Make Your Mark Mindset." If I were reading this book, I would immediately entertain this thought as well. After all, this is probably the main reason you decided to give the book a read in the first place. Given the title, it is likely that you were intrigued by the potential to live a more meaningful life in some way. If this is the case, then you are in luck because this entire book was written with the goal of adding tremendous value to your life. By simply embracing the MYM mindset and the related concepts in the book, you immediately put yourself on a path to realizing three unique benefits that will change your life. While these outcomes tend to overlap and can occur simultaneously, the natural progression is for individuals to pursue them in the order of success, living your best life, and making your mark.

1. SUCCESS. There is a strong likelihood that you picked up this book because you believed it could help you improve your chances of success. It's possible that you are intrigued by the potential to achieve the type financial abundance that will allow you to have far more flexibility in your life. Maybe you would like to live in a dream house or you are interested in completely paying for your kid's college tuition so they can pursue their professional goals. For others, it may not be financially motivated at all and instead has to do with some unique accomplishment you would like to bring to fruition. Regardless of how you define success, the "Make Your Mark Mindset" and the concepts in the book have been written with the sole intention of providing you with the necessary structure to accomplish all of your aspirations. Following the steps outlined in the chapters will put you on the path to achieving remarkable success in key areas of your life.

2. LIVING YOUR BEST LIFE. While society often encourages us to measure success by our external accomplishments, there is another standard that is often far more important to high performers. Make no qualms about it. They absolutely value achieving their goals and having financial abundance in their lives as a priority, but they do not allow it to dictate their lives on a daily basis. Instead, they are focused on performing to their full potential every single day so they can live their absolute best life. Interestingly, this approach is one that leads to massive levels of success even if that end outcome is not a central focus. While this may sound like a vague concept right now, this is a standard that you will come to know well if you invest in the concepts presented in the book on a daily basis. The reason this is a progression is because success, as traditionally defined by our society, does not guarantee that you are living your best life. There are all kinds of people who achieve remarkable levels of success and never feel satisfied with their efforts and/or life. The feeling of happiness they desire often eludes them because they have chosen aspirations that are not in alignment with their core purpose. The whole premise of living your best life is based on realizing your full potential in key areas that are connected to your core inner desires. The good news is you can do exactly this while achieving high levels of success in the areas that matter to you most. This book is designed to inspire and inform you so you can take steps to live your absolute best life.

3. MAKING YOUR MARK. There are very few things in life you cannot achieve if you focus sharply on your vision and consistently making the right investments over extended periods of time to make it a reality. This is the recipe for success that all high performers master as they achieve remarkable things that seem out of reach for most normal people. However, there is another level of accomplishment that you should be aware of as you start on your journey. As you experience success and grow as a person, there will inevitably come a time where you realize that success and personal accomplishments only bring you so much satisfaction. This is when the true make your mark approach comes in to play because you will be ready to learn to live outside of yourself. Not coincidentally, this will be when you realize that the most meaningful aspects of life involve making an impact on the people around us. In the words of the 28th President of the United States Woodrow Wilson, "You are not here merely to make a living. You are here in order to enable the world to live more amply, with greater vision, with a finer spirit of hope and achievement. You are here to enrich the world, and you impoverish yourself if you forget the errand." When you consistently influence lives in a positive manner, you eventually come to a point where you realize that the most meaningful aspects in life are when you learn to add real value to others. It is my belief that you will experience each of these benefits as you invest in the steps laid out throughout this book. Once you start to fully grasp the "Make Your Mark Mindset," you will be ready to achieve extraordinary things that make a lasting impression on people and the world. Remind yourself that it only takes one person's bold actions to drastically change the world.

 You are here to enrich the world, and you impoverish yourself if you forget the errand.
- Woodrow Wilson

The Butterfly Effect

There is a scientific term called "The Butterfly Effect" that refers to small, seemingly inconsequential events that can have large widespread consequences. Coined by a former MIT meteorologist named Edward Lorenz, the scientist proposed a theory that a massive storm could have started from a tiny butterfly flapping its wings in a distant location. This term has made its way into mass culture where it has become a metaphor for smaller, seemingly insignificant moments that drastically change lives and alter the course of history. Not convinced that this applies to humans? Think about the drastic impact that Anne Frank, Mahatma Gandhi, Mother Teresa, Nelson Mandela, and Steve Jobs had on the world because of their actions. While their individual actions may have seemed small at moments in their lives, they eventually compounded and resulted in massive outcomes that altered the course of history. The lesson? You too can make a difference, but you must believe that your actions matter. And not just a little bit. You need to get to the point where you believe that your life is capable of producing an impact comparable to the butterfly described by Lorenz. It's time to get to work so you can fly and cause a chain reaction that results in a lasting impression on the world.

S INEVITABLE. PURSUE THE THING YOU ARE MEANT TO DO ALL OUT AND MAKING YOUR MARK IS INEVITABLE. PURSI

Chapter 1

Adopt the "Make Your Mark" Mindset

> What you do makes a difference, and you have to decide what kind of difference you want to make.
> - Jane Goodall

What if I were to tell you that you have an opportunity to go out and make a remarkable difference in the world? Not a small difference that is virtually unnoticeable to the people around you. What we are talking about here is a real difference that is so distinct that people around you stop and take notice. If you are being completely honest with yourself, is this something you believe you are capable of? If you are representative of the normal population, chances are that you balked at this statement or at least had some negative reaction towards it. It may have been something simple such as a small, subconscious doubt or something far more animated such as thinking I am completely out of my mind. In either instance, your response was negative and you are not sold on the idea that you have the skill sets to go out and impact the world. Before we move on to me explaining why you are flat out wrong in this instance, let's first explore why your response is far more common than you might think.

From the time you were a young child, it is likely that you had people around you that encouraged you to fit in and settle for the status quo. The interesting thing here is that many times the messages from others are so subtle that you don't even recognize what is happening. Maybe you got the courage to tell a friend about your aspirations and rather than responding with support, they said nothing. They certainly did not tell you that it was not possible, but they also did not step up and support you. It is important to note that these reactions are not necessarily intentionally planned to hurt you. However, your brain assesses situations like these and records them as doubt. Chalk another one up for fitting in and toning down your expectations. Interestingly, this happens all the time because most people have also been trained to settle for the status quo. In some instances, these situations are far more blatant where people go out of their way to criticize you and tell you that your aspirations are unfit and unreasonable. Eventually, you have received negative messages like these consistently enough from people and our society in general that you start to doubt your abilities. The shift is so subtle that most people do not even know what has happened. You have been robbed of your ability to dream big and your mind has instead settled for fitting in and playing it safe.

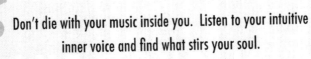

> Don't die with your music inside you. Listen to your intuitive inner voice and find what stirs your soul.
> - @DrWayneWDyer

Remember when I told you that you could go out and make a remarkable impact on the world? It was absolutely true. 100 percent. It is a fact that each of us was put on this earth with unique areas of genius that would allow us to achieve extraordinary things if we utilized them to full potential. Yet most of us never take the time to invest in ourselves to the point where we understand the abilities we have that could impact the people around us. As a result, we never have the opportunity to unveil our gifts to the world. In the words of best selling author Dr. Wayne Dyer, "Don't die with your music still inside you. Listen to your intuitive inner voice and find what passion stirs your soul." It will be a shame if you allow your life to pass without ever pursuing that which you were put on this earth to do. By committing to pursue your highest potential, you give yourself the chance to live an extraordinary life that will make a unique impression on the world. While this may seem like a vague concept at this point, this is exactly what you will learn to do if you fully invest in the concepts presented in this book. However, before we move into specific steps that you can implement to drastically transform your life, it is critical that you start to recruit your mind to get on board with the idea that you can achieve success.

BOARD THE TRAIN TO YOUR BEST LIFE

As you read this book, you have a choice to make when it comes to your life. This is the case regardless of your current situation. You can stay where you are, which may be comfortable, or you can embark on a journey to live your absolute best life, which will likely be uncomfortable at times. If it helps, picture yourself waiting at a train station that is located in a town where you have lived your entire life. You are not particularly thrilled with the town, but you have chosen not to leave because you don't even know where you would go. While it is possible that leaving could lead you to amazing places, there is also the risk that you might end up in a situation that is worse if you embark on a journey to explore new frontiers. Put off by uncertainty, you have chosen to stay put and settle for a life that is comfortable. All of a sudden, a train pulls up that is unlike any other that has previously visited the town. Unlike traditionally colored trains, this one is a pristine gold color with a white trim all around the windows. As it comes to a halt, you notice that the words "BEST LIFE" are printed across the side of the caboose. Intrigued, you walk towards the front of the train and notice that the conductor has hopped out and is walking towards you. As she closes quickly to within five feet of you, she tips her hat and asks, "Will you be joining us today?" Naturally, you respond by asking her where she is headed. With a smile and a sparkle in her eye, she says, "I'm not completely sure, but I have a feeling that it will be someplace special."

When it comes to your life, the situation you are facing is not going to be all that different than the previous train story. No matter where you are currently at in your life, it is always an option for you to travel to a better place if you are willing to step out of your comfort zone and board the train. So, the practical side of you says "what about the part about not knowing the exact end destination?" While that is a perfectly "normal" response, you are going to have to learn to let go of control in this area if you are going to live at your highest level. For now, never mind this presence of self-doubt because the journey is what really matters as you get started. I cannot tell you the exact route that you will take or the end destination where you will arrive. Nobody can and this will be up to you to figure out. I can tell you this though. If you make the decision to board the train and you commit to fully embracing the concepts in this book, you will experience a journey that will drastically change your life. It will truly blow you away. But you must be willing to earn it. All aboard because it is time to go for a ride!

THE STARTING POINT FOR SUCCESS

The journey starts with a subtle shift in your mindset where you choose to pursue excellence in your life. One where you are willing to leap way out of your comfort zone and chase down dreams that most people think are both "unreasonable" and impossible. In many ways, your decision to get on the train is the first step necessary to make this a reality in your life. Deep down, you have a desire to achieve unique accomplishments and this is why you have chosen to read this book. An interesting thing happens once you have made the commitment to live your absolute best life. In the words of best selling author and motivational speaker Robin Sharma, the burning desire to realize your full potential immediately puts you in "rare air" with extraordinary individuals who have had the opportunity to achieve amazing things that have left a lasting impression on the world. While this concept may be foreign to you at this point, and certainly was to me in the past, the good news is that you can learn how to embrace a mindset that will completely transform your life in ways you never previously imagined possible. But first you must accept that there will be no short cuts to your end destination. It will take tremendous investments on your part over extended periods of time to earn the right to live your dreams. With that being said, every second will be worth it if you are willing to make this sacrifice because you will eventually get the chance to make your mark on the world.

DEVELOP AN "EXTRAORDINARY PSYCHOLOGY"

The journey to success always starts with your mindset. Successful people find ways to cultivate an extraordinary mindset that proactively seeks out opportunities to grow on a regular basis. They are committed to assessing each situation they face with a positive outlook so they can find solutions that allow them to advance. Personal development and growth expert Anthony Robbins refers to this approach as an "extraordinary psychology" and explains that this process involves weeding out limiting beliefs and focusing sharply on the positive so you can pursue excellence in all areas of your life. This differentiated psychology has the potential to be born the moment you refuse to settle for status quo and instead cultivate a powerful inner desire to live each day to full potential. This is not a state of being that comes and goes like the tide based on the feelings and challenges life is currently presenting you. No, it is not this at all. Instead, it is an understanding that excellence requires disciplined consistency and a structured lifestyle, where you wake up each morning energized to make each day a masterpiece.

Interestingly, this approach is completely foreign to most people because our society has programmed us to look for the easiest route to success. This instant gratification mentality encourages people to spend their days looking for shortcuts that eventually result in them feeling frustrated and unfulfilled because their approach is destined for failure. They have neglected to comprehend that all meaningful accomplishments are ones that you must earn over time with consistency in your approach and a willingness to sacrifice. There simply are no shortcuts to success because the journey is what makes them so special. When you earn the right to live your dreams, you are blessed with a feeling of real accomplishment because you know deep down inside that you deserve happiness and success. It is not essential that you know how to make this happen at this exact moment, but you must be intrigued by the prospect of changing your life into something unique and memorable so you are willing to take action. In the words of Oprah Winfrey, "We can't become what we need to be by remaining what we are." One of the first steps to implementing change is by developing a remarkable attitude that focuses on the opportunities in your life.

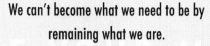

> We can't become what we need to be by
> remaining what we are.
> - Oprah

MAKE POSITIVE A PART OF IT

The first thing you need to understand when striving to develop an extraordinary mindset is that you must learn to focus on the positive in all situations. Thomas Jefferson, an American Founding Father, principal author of the Declaration of Independence, and the third President of the United States explained, "nothing can stop the person with the right mental attitude from achieving their goal; nothing on earth can help the person with the wrong mental attitude." While most people don't realize or accept it, you always have a choice on how you respond to your environment. Unfortunately, research has shown that most people choose negative and use up to 80 percent of their days preoccupied with unproductive thoughts. This means that we waste up to 12.8 hours each day (in an average 16 hour wake period) on counterproductive thoughts that could have been allocated to the pursuit of high priority aspirations. Just imagine all that you could accomplish if you had the self-discipline to adjust your mindset so you could re-allocate these 4,672 hours each year to something more productive. The results would be absolutely staggering!

> " Choose the positive, the constructive. Optimism is
> a faith that leads to success."
> - Bruce Lee

Here is the most important thing for you to recognize when attempting to cultivate an extraordinary psychology. In every situation you face, whether good or bad, it is always within your power to choose exactly what it means to you and how you respond. Legendary martial artist Bruce Lee explained this about the power of choice: "Choose the positive. You have choice - you are master of your attitude - choose the positive, the constructive. Optimism is a faith that leads to success." The most productive people in the world develop the ability to break their interactions down and train themselves to focus on the positive in each situation so they can turn them into opportunities to advance in key areas of their life. Concentration camp survivor and best selling author of *Man's Search for Meaning* Viktor Frankl explains the power that each of us has in our response to our environment: "Between stimulus and response there is space. In that space lies our freedom and power to choose our response. In our response lies our growth and freedom." By working diligently to recognize this space and understanding that there is always a choice, successful people take control of their responses and learn to focus sharply on the positive. Not coincidently, these people tend to attract both the right people and opportunities because they are far more pleasant to be around. This process of focusing on the positive is not an easy one to master, but it is one that is worth the investment because it will dictate what you are able to accomplish in life.

It Will Be Really Tough, But Really Worth It

There is something we should just get out of the way right now. Nothing in this book is designed to teach you about finding an easy route to success. It will certainly be about showing you efficient ways to live at a high level, but you will still have to make the investment to reap the rewards. Simply put, there will be nothing easy about sacrificing and making the daily investments necessary to realize your vision and live to full potential. In fact, in many ways it will be one of the most challenging things you have ever done because it will force you way out of your comfort zone. The iconic Civil Rights leader Martin Luther King Jr. explained this about embracing difficult situations, "The ultimate measure of a person is not where they stand in moments of comfort and convenience, but where they stand at times of challenge." It will take a level of self-discipline that you have likely never mastered in your entire life. There will be adversity and frustrations that will cause you to question your ability to achieve your aspirations. However, if you have the grit to hang in and commit to earning the right to live your dreams, you will come to a point where you experience a life more satisfying than you ever thought possible. The daily investments will eventually compound and the result will be moments of clarity where you have energy and a feeling of confidence that is unparalleled. To get to this point, it is important that you heed the following advice from author and motivational speaker Harvey MacKay: "nobody ever said it would be easy, they just promised that it would be worthwhile."

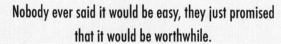

> Nobody ever said it would be easy, they just promised that it would be worthwhile.
> - Harvey MacKay

Expect Daily Doses of Excellence

The part that is most challenging about meaningful success and making your mark on the world is that it takes consistent daily investments. As stated so eloquently by prominent leadership author and speaker Dr. John Maxwell, one of the things that makes life so hard is that it happens every single day. When it comes to extraordinary accomplishments, there simply are no days off. While there will be situations where you are not physically working, there should never be a time where you stray from modeling your values and aspiring to live your best life. The development of an extraordinary mindset is an everyday thing where you are passionate about making consistent investments in yourself. It doesn't matter if you don't feel like it. Once you know exactly how you should be living your life, the goal is to be a master of self-discipline and to become outstanding at implementing your intentions on a daily basis. This is simply another step in the development of an extraordinary psychology that you can capitalize on if you have the right structure in place in your life.

THE COMPOUND EFFECT

In Darren Hardy's *The Compound Effect*, he reiterates the concept of investing in daily doses of excellence when he explains that success is the result of small daily acts that we commit every single day. A common misperception that most people have when it comes to unique accomplishments is that they believe that the outcomes are the result of monumental endeavors that immediately launch fortunate people to success. Jeff Olson, the author of *The Slight Edge*, calls these mystical jumps "quantum leaps" and explains this about meaningful success, "Here is the great secret that holds the key to great accomplishment: both that 'sudden flash' and that 'overnight success' were the final, breakthrough results of a long, patient process of edge upon edge upon edge. Any time you see what looks like a breakthrough, it is always the end result of a long series of little things, done consistently over time. No success is immediate or instantaneous; no collapse is sudden or precipitous." This is exactly why most people are mistaken in their beliefs about success. This edge that he speaks about is the process of investing in the right activities day in and day out for an extended period of time. High performance and extraordinary accomplishments are the result of consistent investments that on the surface appear as if nothing is actually happening. However, if individuals continue to make these investments, their efforts eventually compound over time and they experience this slight edge that transforms their life. It is a mundane, challenging process, but it is one that you must embrace if you are going to reach your full potential in key areas of your life. Given all the challenges that life presents, you will need an uncommon desire to be great if you hope to truly capitalize on this compound effect process.

THE DESIRE TO BE GREAT

We have already made it clear that the process to live your best life is extremely difficult. It is a grinding undertaking where you will be regularly challenged from different angles to abandon your self-discipline. If you are unclear at any point as to why you are investing in the process, then it is likely that these challenges will temporarily overcome you and you will fall back into a lifestyle where you settle for status quo. If you are passionate enough about living to your full potential, this is something that can be avoided with the right approach. When you have tapped into a desire to be great, you will naturally shun the status quo and will charge through even when life presents you with challenges. You certainly have to take steps to preserve the right mindset, which we will discuss in this book, but the end result will be extraordinary if you combine your vision with a growth structure that is conducive to success.

> When you have tapped into a desire to be great, you will naturally shun the status quo.
> - @CoyteCooper

In the groundbreaking book *Think and Grow Rich*, Napoleon Hill studied the most successful people in the world and found that desire was the starting point for all great achievements. This was characterized by a deep inner desire to succeed at a particular task and a willingness to do whatever it took to make it happen. In *Rules of the Red Rubber Ball*, Kevin Carroll explains that, "The desire to follow your red rubber ball [passion] must come from deep within you. The urge should feel irresistible, as if it's percolating up from your soul." Successful people get in touch with this feeling and then spend their days pursuing this "red rubber ball" until it becomes a reality in their physical world. Because it is something that matters deeply to them, they strive to develop the expert skill sets and mindset necessary to make their desire a reality.

Chasing Perfection to Catch Excellence

Legendary National Football League (NFL) coach Vince Lombardi explains that "perfection is not attainable, but if we chase perfection, we can catch excellence." The point to take from this is that you are not perfect, and never will be, but you can reach a crazy high performance level if you have a deep desire to do so and are willing to put in the repetitions to refine your skill sets. As you wake up each day, make it your goal to pursue excellence in your individual interactions so you can make each day a masterpiece. Achieve this by being willing to make consistent daily investments to live your best life. In the words of United States Army four-star general Colin Powell, "If you are going to achieve excellence in big things, you develop the habit in little matters. Excellence is not an exception, it is a prevailing attitude." Develop habits conducive to excellence by always embracing smaller initiatives that are essential to the achievement of your goals and dreams. Hold yourself accountable to these initiatives by putting a structure in place that is conducive to strong self-discipline and confidence in your ability to succeed.

> Perfection is not attainable, but if we chase perfection,
> we can catch excellence.
> - Vince Lombardi

SOLIDIFYING A STRUCTURE TO SUCCEED

Living your best life is a real challenge, but it is one that you can simplify and make possible if you put a structure in place that allows you to cultivate an extraordinary psychology. When you set out to be more positive and proactive in your approach, there will be people around you constantly complaining about situations and problems. This is a part of life. There will be individuals who criticize and question your abilities when you are bold enough to set "unreasonable" dreams and pursue them with a passion. These are normal obstacles that you must be ready to overcome when striving to live an extraordinary life that makes a difference in the world. While we would all love for a positive attitude to come naturally 365 days a year, this is not realistic and our best route for increasing our chances of a positive outlook is putting a daily structure in place that encourages us to focus on opportunities to grow and realize our vision. The most effective way to do this is by investing in a growth system that helps our mind stay focused on achieving extraordinary accomplishments. With the right discipline and commitment to excellence, this system will allow you to put in the repetitions required to live the exact life you desire in the future. We will cover how to implement this system effectively throughout the book.

> A legacy is etched into the minds of others and the
> stories they share about you.
> - Shannon Alder

What Difference Do You Want to Make?

The chapter started with a quote from Jane Goodall explaining that you will make a difference with your actions. You may not currently believe this to be the case, but it is the truth for every person that is put on this earth. Make no mistake about it. Your actions matter and your decisions will influence the people around you in some way. The choice you need to make now is whether or not these impressions are positive or negative. The purpose of the book is to inspire you to land on the positive side of things and strive to make your mark on people every single day. Author Shannon Alder summed this process up best when urging others to "Carve your name on hearts, not tombstones. A legacy is etched into the minds of others and the stories they share about you." It is time for you to decide what stories are going to be told about you. I hope that you will make the wise decision to commit to living your best life and leaving a legacy that makes a lasting impression on the world.

NORMAN BOURLAG

Norman Bourlag, awarded the Noble Peace Prize in 1970 for a lifetime of work feeding hungry people, was a person who was able to leave a lasting impression on the world because of his actions. Raised in Cresco, Iowa, Dr. Bourlag had a passion for farming that led him to earning his Ph.D. in Plant Pathology from the University of Minnesota in 1942. Following his graduation, he participated in the Rockefeller Foundation's pioneering technical assistance program in Mexico where he served as a research scientist in charge of solving wheat problems that limited food production. This work led him to developing a high-yielding, disease resistant wheat that was able to grow effectively in countries across the world where people were dying due to starvation. This provided a stable food source that was critical for saving lives across the world. In total, Dr. Bourlag was credited with saving over one billion lives and made a mark that will always be remembered.

KEY SUMMARY POINTS

O   An extraordinary mindset is absolutely essential to success. You must embrace a positive mindset that allows you to use all of the minutes in your day to pursue your dreams.

O   Nothing about living your best life is going to be easy. The most meaningful accomplishments in life are ones that you must earn and this will require you to embrace being uncomfortable in your approach.

O   Success requires daily doses of excellence that will compound over time and transform your life. This demands a consistent approach where you are willing to do the "little things" even when you don't feel like it.

O   Your ability to achieve great things will be dictated by your daily habits. The willingness to implement a structure conducive to success will drastically increase your chances of success and making your mark on the world.

CHAPTER 2

DARE TO DREAM WAY BEYOND "REASONABLE" EXPECTATIONS

> "You will find that there are no limits to what you can accomplish except for the limits you place on your imagination. And since there are no limits to what you can imagine, there are no limits to what you can achieve. This is one of the greatest discoveries of all."
> -Brian Tracy

ONE OF THE greatest gifts that you have been given as a human being is your ability to dream of all the things you would like to accomplish in your life. Author and speaker Dr. Myles Munroe explains that this is referred to as vision and it encompasses the ability to take a trip to the future to see all the things you want to accomplish, and then returning to the present to make plans to go there. The fascinating thing about vision is that the human race is one of the only species on this planet with the ability to think intelligently about the future. In the words of Daniel Gilbert, the Harvard psychologist and author of *Stumbling on Happiness*, "We [humans] think about the future in a way that no other animal can, does, or ever has, and this simple, ubiquitous, ordinary act is a defining feature of our humanity." Interestingly, despite having this rare gift, only a small percentage of people ever take advantage of their ability to form a long-term vision that they are truly passionate about. In fact, research has shown that only three percent of people actually write down their goals and revisit them on a regular basis. This is potentially one of the most unfortunate statistics you will ever find because it means that most people will never actually realize their dreams and have the experience of living with real passion.

The Incredible Value of Vision

Living without energy and purpose is the most alarming outcome for individuals who lack vision in their life. However, there is another tangible consequence that often grabs people's attention when they learn about it. According to Dr. Edward Banfield, formerly a scholar at Harvard University, long-term perspective (vision) was the single most important factor when attempting to determine why individuals experience meaningful success. It was deemed more essential than education, family background, intelligence, and influential contacts. The take home finding here was that not having a vision dramatically decreases people's chances of success. If you are not convinced of the validity of this study, it is important to point out that this research has been regularly reinforced by other experts in the field studying human performance and success. Even more intriguing has been the information that has emerged on exactly how much a lack of vision can impact people. How much could this possibly cost you? I think you will be more than a little shocked to learn the answer as you read about the "3/97 Rule of Vision."

The 3/97 Rule of Vision

We have already addressed the fact that long-term vision is a critical component to realizing success. But longer-term vision (10+ years) is not the only element to consider when pursuing lofty aspirations. Once this is in place, it is necessary to track back to identify shorter-term goals that provide a roadmap to realize your longer-term vision. How important exactly? In his book *What They Don't Teach You at Harvard Business School*, Mark McCormack outlines a 10-year study at Harvard University that focused on the importance of setting goals among MBA students. In an initial analysis, data demonstrated that only 13% of the graduates had goals, and of these individuals, only three percent had written them down and made definite plans to achieve them. While these statistics alone are fascinating, the most impactful findings came when they followed up with these same participants 10 years later. In the follow-up assessment, the researchers found that the three percent of graduates who wrote down their goals out earned the remaining 97 percent of graduates combined. While earning potential is certainly not the only meaningful measure of success, the findings certainly shed light onto the importance of utilizing our gift of vision and the ability to plan our future.

> "The three percent of graduates who wrote down their goals out earned the remaining 97 percent of graduates."
> -Mark McCormack

So, Why Don't People Dream?

If you are anything like me, the first thing you wonder when seeing the statistics on vision and long-term planning is "why the heck don't people set goals?" If there is so much at stake, it makes no sense that people would not take the time to identify where they would like to go someday and how they plan to get there. The reality is that only three percent of all people invest the time to revisit their longer-term aspirations on a daily basis. There are some primary reasons why this is the case. It is important that you understand these limitations so you can identify what is holding you back from writing down your vision and living to full potential. Without further ado, I present to you five common factors that most commonly influence people's ability to dream.

1. DON'T KNOW WHAT YOU DON'T KNOW. One of the main reasons why people don't invest in vision and goal setting is that they have no clue how important this process is to their future success. Even with proactive people, many of them have never learned about long-term planning and how essential it is to achieving unique accomplishments in life. Without them even knowing it, they have failed to place themselves in the top three percent of high performing individuals who run laps around the remaining 97 percent of the field. Now that you know the consequences of a lack of vision, this will not be an issue. Simply follow through on the steps outlined in the book to drastically increase your chances of success.

2. NOT SURE HOW TO GET STARTED. Even when people learn about the "3/97 Rule of Vision," it can often be difficult for them to get the process moving because they do not know where to start. While most people have a general concept of what a goal is, very few actually know exactly what they should look like in a tangible form that relates to their life. As a result, research has shown that they are only using two percent of their mental capacity because they have not learned how to challenge themselves in ways that allow them to reach full potential. If you want to put yourself in the top tier of elite performers, you must commit to becoming highly efficient at setting goals that are in direct alignment with your vision. This is a process you will have the opportunity to master as you move through this book.

3. FEAR OF FAILURE AND DISCOMFORT. If simply comprehending the importance of long-term planning was all that was needed to drastically alter human performance, it is safe to say that most people would likely take the time to write down and revisit their vision and goals. However, there are some other real obstacles that deter people from investing in this long-term planning process. At the top of this list for most people is the fear of failure and discomfort. Even when people learn about the implications of long-term planning, they often consciously or unconsciously make the decision to refrain from setting goals because they are afraid of what they will look like to others if they fall short of expectations. Or they avoid investing in the process because they intuitively know what it will take to achieve lofty aspirations. In other words, they take themselves "out of the game" because they have no interest in living outside of their comfort zone. The problem with both of these approaches is that they limit individuals from ever reaching their full potential because they are playing it safe. They are choosing comfortable. If you want to achieve unique accomplishments with your life, you must identify when this response occurs for you and then commit to getting out of your comfort zone. This step is a requirement for being in the top three percent of elite performers.

4. LACK OF DISCIPLINE. In my experience of working with people, there are individuals who grasp the importance of setting goals and accept the fact that they need to step outside of their comfort zone to make their dreams a reality. Yet when they return to their normal daily routine, they end up getting distracted and never follow through on their intentions. This is when you quickly learn that there is another essential step that you need to take if you are going to be successful in the long-term planning process. While it is not a difficult process to comprehend, you still need to be able to sit down, block out all the clutter around you, and spend the energy necessary to comprehend the vision and goals that inspire you to take action. Interestingly, this is the step that most often holds people back because it takes self-discipline and this tends to be scarce in our society. It is not easy to immediately know the things that you are passionate about because it takes time to reflect on your inner values. You must be willing to invest in yourself over extended periods of time and to reflect on the growth process so you gain an understanding of the vision and goals that inspire you. When you earn the right to understand these areas, you will be ready to take steps to live your best life and to make your mark on the world.

> "The ones who are crazy enough to think that they can change the world, are the ones who do."
> -Steve Jobs

5. NEGATIVE INFLUENCE OF SOCIETY. On top of all of the previous reasons, there is a final factor that always comes into play when it comes to learning to dream beyond normal expectations. The reason that most people don't know how to cast vision or choose not to is because our society teaches us to settle for the status quo. From a young age, we are encouraged to do whatever it takes to simply fit in and not do anything to stand out from the crowd. The crazy thing is that these lessons often come from people who should be teaching us how to set remarkably high standards for our life. By the time we get into our teenage years, we have lost the ability to dream and set goals. If you want to become a top performer, you need to reprogram your mind to dream big and not worry about what other people think about your aspirations. It is inevitable that people will think that your approach is "unreasonable" if you set extremely high standards and pursue your best life. In these instances, remind yourself that all extraordinary accomplishments are considered "unreasonable" by most people's standards. In the words of the legendary Apple founder Steve Jobs, "the ones who are crazy enough to think that they can change the world, are the ones who do." Be one of the few crazy enough to make this happen.

COMMIT TO LIVING THE DREAM!

If you want to avoid the previous pitfalls and live your best life, you need to commit to "living the dream" today. Even if you don't know what your vision and goals are at the moment, it is essential that you determine right now that you will commit to finding dreams that you hope to pursue in your life. When it matters enough to you to overcome society's negative influence, lack of discipline, and the fear of discomfort, you will be ready to begin your journey to earn the right to live your dreams. It is at this point that you must understand that identifying dreams that are connected to your purpose, passions, and areas of genius can take time. You will need to be willing to invest in personal growth and reflection so you choose a vision that is in alignment with the things that truly matter to you as a person. Before we begin this journey, let's first explore some common perceptions of success so you get on the right path to realizing your full potential.

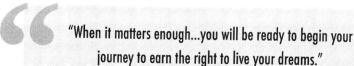

> "When it matters enough...you will be ready to begin your journey to earn the right to live your dreams."
> -@coytecooper

COMMON MISPERCEPTION OF SUCCESS

The mistake many people make is that they think that success is reserved for select people with unique skill sets and/or situations. Their assessment here is actually both correct and incorrect, but it is not in the way that you would initially think. They are correct that success can be influenced by unique gifts that a person has been blessed with. However, this is only a part of the process as these individuals have also made investments to nurture their one-of-a-kind skill sets so they can live out their purpose. On the other hand, these individuals are also incorrect in their assessment of success because they are assuming that they do not have their own unique gifts that would allow them to achieve extraordinary things. While they are often not the same as the people they are comparing themselves to on a regular basis, each person was put on this earth with abilities that will allow them to realize meaningful success if they are in alignment with their purpose. Your job is to find these gifts so you can unveil them to the world en route to living your dreams.

How You Can Start to Live the Dream

Before we touch on specific steps you can take to live the dream, let's first provide an explanation of exactly what a dream is and how it can influence your life. Business consultant Robert Kriegel eloquently described them when explaining, "A dream is an ideal involving a sense of possibilities, of potential rather than limits. A dream is the wellspring of passion, giving us direction and pointing us to lofty heights. It is an expression of optimism, hope, and values lofty enough to capture the imagination and engage the spirit. Dreams grab us and move us. They are capable of lifting us to new heights and overcoming self-imposed limitations." In essence, a dream is a future vision that taps in to our passions and gives us a reason to live our days all out. When you find your dream, you will know because it will energize you and inspire you to become a much better person. Again, the key is investing in yourself on a daily basis and reflecting so you can learn the things that you are passionate about.

So, are you ready to take steps to live the dream? I sure hope so because we are ready to get down to business. The single most important thing that you can do to start living the dream is to take immediate action to move toward full potential today. This starts with the investment in growth initiatives that will allow you to develop as a person so you understand your gifts and areas that move you emotionally. The commitment to move towards an extraordinary life is a foundational element because it is inevitable that you will grow when you take action and learn from repetition. If this seems vague at this point, continue to read on because the "Six Initial Steps to Live the Dream" outlined in the chapter will get you moving in the right direction. These are meant to simply provide you with a starting point for you to explore this process of vision. In no way are these designed to provide you with all the answers to your journey right now. Rather, they will allow you to form some initial thoughts that will be developed as you move throughout the book. Hopefully they will be the seeds for an extraordinary life for you in the future!

> "The two most important days in your life are the day you were born and the day you find out why."
> -Mark Twain

STEP 1 - CREATE CLARITY IN YOUR PURPOSE. While it might sound corny to you now, we all have a specific thing we are meant to do that will allow us to make our mark on the world. When discussing the relevance of purpose, the legendary author Mark Twain explained, "The two most important days in your life are the day you were born and the day you find out why." Here is the challenging part. Nobody can tell you what this is for you because this is something that is unique to your being. It is something that comes from a willingness to constantly grow and reflect on the experiences that come from living life to the fullest each day. If you are willing to get out of your comfort zone and pursue your passions, there will come a day when you know exactly what you were meant to do with your life. When this day comes, there will be a clarity in your approach that energizes you to use every minute of your day proactively to pursue your vision. This is when you need to capitalize on your unique skill sets to make sure you have a path that allows you to perform at an elite level.

STEP 2 - FIND YOUR AREAS OF GENIUS. If purpose is the specific reason you were put on this earth, then your unique skill sets are the gifts that you have been given to help make this purpose a reality. Here is the tricky part. As with most of the other areas in this book, it is entirely up to you to gain an understanding of these "areas of genius" so you can nurture them in a way that will allow you to pursue your purpose and realize your dreams. Simply put, these are areas where you can shine and contribute to the world in a way that few other people can. As explained by bestselling author Napoleon Hill, "Just as a master musician may cause the most beautiful strains of music to pour forth from the strings of a violin, so may you arouse the genius which lies asleep in your brain, and cause it to drive you upward to whatever goal you may wish to achieve." It can take time to know exactly what your "areas of geniuses" are, but it is worth the investment because they will provide you with an opportunity to perform at your highest level on a regular basis. There are few things more satisfying than knowing you are living to your absolute full potential and your "areas of genius" represent the breeding grounds to make this a reality. These also happen to be the areas where you will find your passion points because you will be realizing your full potential.

STEP 3 - PURSUE YOUR PASSION POINTS. It is not enough for you to simply find ways to use your areas of genius. After all, this will eventually lose its appeal if you are engaging in activities that are not in alignment with your passion points. But what the heck are passion points exactly? These are characterized by the activities that energize and excite you because they are in alignment with your inner desires. If you notice that you feel inspired when you get the chance to implement customer service initiatives, then there is a good chance that you are passionate about working with people and adding value to their lives. When you understand these passion points, then you can make decisions in your life to ensure you are working in areas that connect you with your purpose. These are areas that will keep you fully engaged even when you are facing adversity because they are in alignment with your core desires. This is exactly what makes highly successful people unique. They are efficient at identifying passion points that are in direct alignment with their vision.

> "You have to be willing to dream big and take steps even when you cannot see the entire staircase."
> -@coytecooper

STEP 4 - SOLIDIFY AN "UNREASONABLE" VISION. For efficiency purposes, it makes sense that you first gain an understanding of your purpose, areas of genius, and passion points prior to putting a vision in place for your life. Because these deal with your unique skill sets and the areas that inspire you, they will serve as a critical guide to make sure you choose a path where you can both perform at an elite level and make an impact on the world. If you have not already gathered, your vision is a view of exactly where you would like to go and what you would like to accomplish in your life. As you consider putting a vision in place, remind yourself that you only get one chance to live this life so you might as well strive to set extraordinary expectations. While your vision will evolve as you develop as a person, it is important that your initial aspirations are bold enough that they force you outside of your comfort zone. If there are people around you that think you are being "unreasonable," then you are on the right track because you have likely set a vision that is challenging enough, and this is the type of expectation that will put you on the path to success. That is, as long as you are willing to put in the work each day and do the things that are necessary to earn the right to live this vision. You don't have to know exactly how to get there, but you have to be willing to dream big and take steps even when you cannot see the entire staircase.

STEP 5 - INVEST IN A VALUE SYSTEM. While you will not always know what the next step will be in the pursuit of your vision, you can certainly identify principles that are necessary to realize your dreams. If your goal is to become a CEO in the future, then there are attributes that you need to cultivate to maximize the chances that you realize your aspirations. For example, it would not take much time researching top CEO's to understand that integrity is a critical value if you are going to lead people effectively. In fact, it is essential that you learn to model this exceptionally well because it will determine your ability to connect with people and get them on board to support your vision. As explained in my *Impressions* book, values can be defined as the core beliefs and philosophies that are most important to us in our life, and they guide our daily decisions to ensure authenticity in our approach. Successful people know the values that matter to them most and they put a structure in place to live them each day so they can realize full potential. The identification of values also allows them to choose principles that are in alignment with their long-term philosophy and planning.

STEP 6. ALIGN YOUR PURPOSE, GENIUS, PASSIONS, VISION, AND VALUES. The gold standard in elite personal performance and living an extraordinary life is taking the time to know your purpose, areas of genius, passions, vision, and values so you can do everything possible to make sure they are in alignment. When what you are good at (areas of genius) and what you care about (passions) are in alignment with your vision, you give yourself an opportunity to perform at a truly elite level because you have created a path that you are meant to master. Once you know this path, it is simply about understanding some of the principles (values) you need to embrace to allow your full potential to unveil itself during your journey. When each of these pieces are in place, it is just a matter of time until the reason you were put on this earth (purpose) becomes clear to you. If you are able to achieve complete alignment in these five areas, you will cultivate a feeling of calm and happiness because you will be living the exact life you are meant to be living. The result will be extraordinary accomplishments that you never previously thought possible.

Being Unsure is Normal as You Start

As you read through the steps, it is highly likely that you were not immediately clear on how to proceed. Just know that this is a normal response because these are inner foundational areas that will take time to fully understand. Many of the steps are going to take a significant investment (time and energy) to master because they will require consistent personal development and reflection over extended periods of time. When it comes to understanding your inner self, it is important to acknowledge that there will be no short cuts and you need to plan on embracing the journey that comes with living your best life. It all starts with being willing to push forward and take action when you are unsure how it is going to unfold. This is exactly what highly successful people do on a regular basis. They take immediate steps to make things happen while others sit around contemplating all the reasons why they shouldn't do something or why they won't work out.

If you want to be different than these people and live a life that is worth remembering, you need to embrace uncertainty and teach yourself to be excited about taking consistent steps towards the pursuit of your dreams.

RE-LEARNING TO DREAM LIKE A KID

Best selling author Robin Sharma regularly talks about children and how they come to us far more highly evolved than adults to teach us the lessons we need to learn. When it comes to dreaming big, this is absolutely the case. To illustrate this point, close your eyes and take a trip back to when you were a kid and think about the things that you dreamed about. As you picture these things, try to remember exactly how they made you feel. I don't know about you, but the dreams that I had (e.g., State Champion) energized me and kept me moving throughout my day. I can even remember acting them out with my brother in our garage and truly believing they would happen. If you can remember this, then you know exactly what it means to re-learn to dream like a kid. It is not important that your dreams are the same as they were when you were younger. In fact, it is almost certain that they will be different because you are hopefully a more evolved person. The important thing is that you learn to allow your mind to run wild thinking about all of the things you would like to achieve in your life. Don't be frustrated if this is challenging to do at the start because it is likely that you have not used this ability in a long time. It is just like a muscle in that you need to work it regularly to strengthen it. Eventually, if you have the discipline to visualize this process on a daily basis, your mind will naturally start to dream about the specific things you are passionate about accomplishing.

TAKE REGULAR TRIPS TO THE FUTURE

When you come upon your dream, you will know because it will energize you when you think about it. The thought of being able to live your dream will excite you and inspire you to take immediate action to make it a reality. However, you cannot expect to keep this energy without working to stay connected to your vision. To ensure that this happens, you should build in time on a regular basis to take trips to the future. Ideally, you would do this on a daily basis, but at minimum you should do it once a week as you start your week. Set aside time (5-10 minutes) and find a quiet place where you can visualize yourself achieving your dream and living to full potential. Specifically see yourself living the exact life you would like to live and be as detailed as possible. Once your time is up, take the advice of bestselling author Dr. Myles Munroe and come back to the present and make specific plans to go there. At this point, it is your job to be bold enough to follow through on your intentions and make sure that your mind is an ally as you embark on the journey to achieve your dreams.

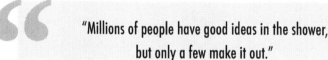

"Millions of people have good ideas in the shower, but only a few make it out."
-Dr. John C Maxwell

FOLLOWING THROUGH ON YOUR INTENTIONS

Once you have established the dream of what you would like to achieve with your life, the journey has just begun because you need to follow through with all of your intentions. And there is nothing easy about this because following through on your intentions takes discipline, persistence, and hard work. Which is exactly why so few people actually follow through and achieve their dreams. In the words of leadership guru Dr. John Maxwell, "Millions of people have good ideas in the shower, but only a few will make it out." If you want to be a part of the rare group of people who live their dreams, then you need to commit to getting out of your comfort zone and growing on a regular basis. The art of following through and demonstrating discipline around your fundamentals each day will serve as the foundation for all of your future achievements.

LEARN TO MAKE YOUR MIND AN ALLY

As you embark on your journey to live your dreams, there will come times where you question your ability to achieve them. This may come from outside criticism of others who feel you are being "unreasonable" or it may simply be a time where you are facing adversity and your vision is cloudy. Regardless of why you are feeling this way, this is exactly when you need to tell your mind to be quiet and instead redirect it to focus sharply on your vision. If you have a solid structure in place that clearly outlines where you are going, then this will be much easier to accomplish. The good news is that we will cover this throughout the book. If you do not have a structure in place yet, then simply keep reading and investing in yourself until your vision becomes crystal clear. Another strategy is to simply quiet your mind and repeat the mantra "earn the right to live your dream" until you are refocused and ready to move forward in a more productive manner. The bottom line is that you have to make sure that your mind is on board to help you achieve all of your dreams.

FIND THE PROACTIVE VOICE WITHIN YOU

There is going to be a part of your journey that involves finding the proactive voice within you. This is a voice that tells you things that will allow you to know your purpose and what you were put on this earth to do. The challenge will be that your voice has likely been taught to be quiet as you were trained to settle for the status quo throughout your life. As you explore the things you are passionate about, eventually a proactive voice will emerge that will guide you if you are diligent enough to listen for it. In *Live Your Dreams*, Les Brown explains this about your inner voice: "Find that voice in yourself. Look deep into yourself for it. If others don't hear it, that's okay. It is there in you. It is there in all of us. We all have a driving force within us. Keep in mind that when you hear those encouraging voices, you must listen to them and ignore all logic. Mere logic does not always work." The important thing is to learn to block out the negative and trust this proactive voice so you are able to fully pursue your dreams with a clear mind.

Go "Ollin" and Be One of Few to Live the Dream

In Kevin Hall's *Aspire*, he touches on an Ancient Aztec word called "Ollin" that means to "act and move with all of your heart." If you want the opportunity to reach full potential and to live your best life, then you need to go "Ollin" when pursuing your dreams. When you know exactly where you want to go with you life, your job is to act and move with all your heart to make it a reality. The first step is simply making the decision that you are fully committed to living your best life, and that you will not allow any distractions or excuses to get you off track. Now that you are ready to make this happen, it is time to move through some steps you can take to realize all of your dreams and make your mark on the world. We will start with solidifying a growth structure that will set you up for lasting success in the future.

ANTHONY ROBLES

There are people in this world that dream beyond all expectations and Anthony Robles is one of them. Born in 1988, Robles came into the world without his right leg and doctors could not explain what went wrong or why he was missing a leg. Despite this set back, his mom continuously strived to instill confidence by telling him he was made this way for a reason and that he could achieve whatever he set his mind to. After joining the middle school wrestling team at 14, his record at the end of his first year was 5-8 and he finished in last place in the Mesa City Wresting Tournament. However, Anthony was not deterred and he set his mind to becoming an elite wrestler. Eventually, he realized his dream as he went on to a 96-0 record and won two state championships for Mesa High School. On top of this, he won a high school national championship. Despite his credentials, college coaches did not want to take a chance on Anthony because of his size and "perceived" limitations. Did this stop Anthony? Not one bit! Believing they were wrong in their assessment of his abilities, he walked on at Arizona State and became a 3x NCAA All-American and National Champion. In the process, he won over all kinds of supporters because of his kindness and his amazing ability to dream. Anthony Robles is an extraordinary example of what you can achieve when you have a clear vision and you go "Ollin" to make it happen.

KEY SUMMARY POINTS

O   Strive to immediately put yourself in the top three percent of elite performers by exploring your dreams and putting them to paper. You can immediately differentiate yourself and increase your chances of success by simply writing your dreams down.

O   Fight off all the negative influences around you and take steps today to live the dream. The six steps presented in the chapter will help increase your chances of maintaining a position in the three percent of elite performers.

O   Re-learn to dream like a kid and take regular trips to the future to see your vision. You can drastically increase your chances of success if you cultivate your ability to dream.

O   Go "Ollin" and fully pursue your vision so you have the opportunity to realize your dreams, live your best life, and make your mark on the world. You cannot do this if you do not fully commit to the process required to make your mark on the world.

S INEVITABLE. PURSUE THE THING YOU ARE MEANT TO DO ALL OUT AND MAKING YOUR MARK IS INEVITABLE. PURS

Chapter 3

Solidify a Growth System for Lasting Success

> " We are what we repeatedly do. Excellence, therefore, is not an act but a habit. "
>
> -Aristotle

ONE OF THE biggest mistakes that many people make is thinking that success is reserved for someone else. This is in large part because we are taught at a young age to fit in and settle for the status quo. At some point, whether intentional or not, we are trained to believe that we do not deserve to achieve extraordinary things because we are inadequate in some way. Or we are led to believe that success is only meant for other people who are born with natural talents or into better environments. This could not be further from the truth. In fact, previous research has continuously proven that meaningful accomplishments are instead the result of decisions that are made by individuals to live their lives in a unique manner each day. As illustrated by Aristotle in the opening quote, excellence is earned by solid habits that you form over time based on your daily decisions. One of the best ways to ensure that you develop habits that are conducive to success and realizing your dreams is by developing a structure that allows you to move progressively towards full potential. If you don't commit to doing this, you are essentially leaving your future outcome to chance.

Avoid the "Roll the Dice" Approach

The best advice you can get when it comes to success and living your best life is to never leave it to chance. Your life is not a game of craps where you roll the dice and hope for a favorable outcome. If it is, then you can expect to be disappointed with your results at least half of the time. This is actually the approach most people take with their lives as they move through each day without a plan hoping for good things to happen. If they were playing darts, this would be the equivalent of being blindfolded and spun around ten times before taking aim to hit the bulls eye. Because they have no organized approach to their life, they have little chance to ever achieve meaningful success. The good news is that you can eliminate chance and maximize your chances of living a great life if you are just willing to implement a growth system that is conducive to high performance. In the words of leadership expert Dr. John Maxwell, "You will never change your life until you change something you do daily. The secret to your success is found in your daily routine."

Committing To an Effective Growth System

There are few things more powerful than investing in a daily growth system when it comes to success. If you have a lofty vision and goals, you are going to be forced to step way out of your comfort zone to make them a reality. Because these long-term aspirations will likely include skill sets that you don't yet have, it is going to be essential that you find ways to maximize growth on a daily basis. The challenge is that most people have extremely busy schedules and they do not believe that they have time to invest in personal growth initiatives. If this is your current mindset, then consider the fact that strategic growth in key areas will allow you to be far more efficient with your time each day. It is guaranteed that a small investment of 30 minutes of your time each day to work on yourself will bring a much larger return to your productivity and life. If you still feel that your day is too booked up to make this happen, then commit to getting up 30 to 60 minutes early each day and get your day started on a productive note. In regard to this early morning routine, former author and editor of the Saturday Evening Post George Lorimer explained, "You've got to get up each morning with determination if you want to go to bed with satisfaction." If you are still not sold on this concept, then read on and consider all the benefits of becoming an "early riser."

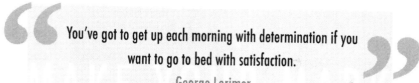

> "You've got to get up each morning with determination if you want to go to bed with satisfaction.
> -George Lorimer

BECOME AN EARLY RISER

One of the things that nearly all of the top performance coaches in the world have in common is their insistence on people getting up early to work on themselves. There are a couple key reasons why this is the case. Bestselling author and elite performance expert Anthony Robbins calls the early morning investment the "Hour of Power" and explains that getting up early will energize you and give you a feeling of confidence that will transform your life. Success coach Robin Sharma refers to the process as "Joining the 5 O'clock Club" and explains that getting up early is the ideal time to feed your mind and nourish your soul on your way to your best life. On top of this, the decision to get up early and invest in a growth system will set the tone for your day as it will train your mind to focus on the positive. This will ensure a proactive approach as you head off each morning to pursue your dreams.

WINNING THE "BATTLE OF THE BED"

No matter who you are, there will be times when you hear your alarm go off and you consider staying in bed for a split second. This may actually be a regular battle that you have with your mind every single day as you strive to make waking up early a habit. In the words of General George S. Patton, "Now if you are going to win any battle you have to do one thing. You have to make the mind run the body. Never let the body tell the mind what to do. The body will always give up. It is always tired in the morning, noon, and night. But the body is never tired if the mind is not tired." If you are going to win the "battle of the bed," you must train your mind to look forward to the opportunity to get up and earn the right to live your dreams. When the alarm clock goes off, you need to jump out of bed and get moving right away regardless of how your body feels. Eventually, this will become easier as you transition into a normal morning routine.

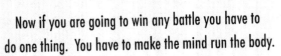

Now if you are going to win any battle you have to do one thing. You have to make the mind run the body.

-George S. Patton

THE MAGIC OF A MORNING ROUTINE

Once you are committed to joining the "5 O'clock Club," the next step is to put a plan in place so you know exactly how you are going to use your time. This is a critical element because it will set the tone for the benefits that you realize in the immediate and long-term future. If you are not clear about your routine, then you are far more likely to see the decision to get up early as a waste of time and it will only be a matter of time until you make the decision to stay in bed and get more sleep. However, if you are efficient with your approach and put a sound growth system in place, it will energize you and your efforts will compound over time. In fact, as you consistently invest in the right activities over a period of weeks and months, it is likely that you will want to progress with your efforts and add more initiatives to your morning routine. This will turn your "30 Minutes to Transform" into an "Hour of Power" and you will take a giant leap towards living your best life.

The great thing about growth is that it does not have to be complicated. In fact, it can actually be a simple and fairly straightforward process if you are investing in the right initiatives. However, it is important to point out that the simplicity in the planning phase does not mean that implementation will be easy. This is clearly illustrated by the fact that most people know things in their life they should be doing, but few actually follow through and make them happen. We will outline five progression growth initiatives with the potential to drastically transform your life, but it will be entirely up to you to follow through and make them a regular part of your growth system. If you are effective at following through and making them a habit, you will eventually start to accomplish things that you never previously thought possible. For now, commit to waking up each morning and giving 30 minutes to the first progression initiative. If you would like to make a larger commitment to your growth system, then simply add initiatives to your routine. However, remember that consistency is the most critical element to growth so make sure you don't bite off more than you can handle as you get started.

PROGRESSION #1: READ THE RIGHT BOOKS. There are few things more powerful than reading the right types of books on a regular basis. On any given day, you have an opportunity to learn from the best people in the world who have achieved extraordinary accomplishments in their lives. If you love autobiographies, then you can learn from legendary past leaders such as: Abraham Lincoln, Amelia Earhart, Hellen Keller, Mahatma Gandhi, Nelson Mandela, Steve Jobs, Thomas Edison, Walt Disney, and/or Winston Churchill. On the topic of personal development and growth, you have the opportunity to read books from authors such as Andy Andrews, Anthony Robbins, Brian Tracy, Gretchen Rubin, Jack Canfield, John Maxwell, Robin Sharma, and a host of other individuals who can help transform your life. All you have to do is commit to developing a reading list and then sitting down 30 minutes each day during your morning routine to put in the repetitions. While this does require a small financial investment, the upside is tremendous as it can transform your life in ways your never previously thought possible. And all you have to do is commit to reading the right books for 30 minutes each day!

PROGRESSION #2: GET IN THE HABIT OF JOURNALING. As you invest in a reading routine, you will regularly have thoughts that stimulate your mind and have the potential to impact your future success. One of the best ways to capture these thoughts so you can revisit them is by writing in a journal each day. In addition to being a repository for your most important thoughts, the simple act of writing things down starts the process of depositing critical information into your mind and activating your subconscious mind. In *Blink: The Power of Thinking Without Thinking*, author Malcom Gladwell refers to this process as "thin splicing" and explains that our mind becomes more efficient at making instant decisions with more quality repetitions. Journaling is an ideal opportunity to place the right types of information and thoughts into your mind. In addition, you can use this process to reflect on your performance and identify strategies to improve your efforts moving forward. This is the second progression because it naturally fits with reading the right books each day. If you are struggling with what to write in your journal as you get started, then you can simply reflect on the key lessons you are learning about in books and how they can impact your life. Another step will be writing about your vision, goals, and values that you will put into place as you read through this book.

PROGRESSION #3: REVISIT VISION, GOALS, AND VALUES. One of the essential things you must do if you are going to achieve success, live an extraordinary life, and make your mark on the world is to revisit your vision, goals, and values on regular basis. As you progress in your morning routine, you will likely be inspired to add key elements to extend growth because you will recognize the benefits being realized in your life. The additional time investment that you previously thought unreasonable will no longer be an issue because you will recognize that five to ten minutes each day is worth the opportunity to transform your life. But before you can follow through on revisiting them each day, you must first be willing to invest time so there is clarity in your vision, goals, and values. This clarity will allow you to know the exact type of person that you hope to become in the future.

> "There is something amazing about investing and truly believing you deserve the right to live your dreams.
> -@coytecooper

PROGRESSION #4: VISUALIZE YOURSELF ACHIEVING YOUR DREAMS. We have already touched on the importance of visualizing yourself achieving your goals and dreams. This process is critical because it allows you to regularly envision where you would like to go in the future. The amazing thing about the subconscious mind is that it does not know the difference between the things you visualize and the things that are a reality at the moment. So, if you learn to visualize your aspirations in great detail, it is training your subconscious mind to believe it is a reality and it is only a matter of time until they occur. Another critical element is the repetition of the process because it will build confidence in your ability to achieve extraordinary things. There is something amazing about investing and truly believing you deserve the right to live your dreams. Visualization is a key part of achieving your aspirations so you should strive to incorporate it as you move through your growth system progressions.

PROGRESSION #5: COMMIT TO EXERCISING AND EATING WELL. Lofty dreams and goals take lofty investments. And often this investment will require large reserves of energy so you can maximize the efficiency of each day. It will be impossible for you to achieve extraordinary things and live your best life if you are tired all the time. The good news is the previous growth progressions will instill a newfound energy into your life. Once they become habit, your confidence will soar and you will look forward to getting up early each morning to charge through your routine. To compound efforts, you will need to make sure you are taking care of your body as well. There is no better way to do this than making sure that you are exercising for 20-30 minutes on a regular basis. While there are different workout plans that you can implement, the point is that you need to make a habit of being active so you can tap into new energy that will transform your life. Similarly, you can do everything else right and still be tired if you put the wrong foods into your body. The key here is to commit to fueling your body with high-energy drinks and food so you can move through your day with a vibrancy that will make your life extraordinary.

PRACTICE PROGRESSION IN EFFORTS

One of the keys to success when developing a growth system

is learning to progress in your efforts. While we would all love to immediately jump in and fully embrace an in-depth growth program, the reality is that we sometimes have to start with steps to make sure we are ready to establish long-term habits. If you bite off too much at one time, you run the risk of becoming frustrated and failing with your efforts. Remind yourself that the goal is to give yourself a chance to develop world-class self-discipline over time. To do this, you must choose an approach that you can follow through on every single day as you get started. This is why the best route is to start with the first two progressions of reading 30 minutes and journaling to reflect on your thoughts as you start each day. Once you have done this for a couple of months and it has become engrained as a habit you look forward to, you are ready to move on to the next progression. Continue to do this until you have a morning growth routine in place that is conducive to achieving all of your goals and dreams.

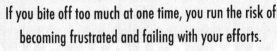

If you bite off too much at one time, you run the risk of becoming frustrated and failing with your efforts.

-@coytecooper

DAILY DOSES OF DISCIPLINE

The development of a growth system is about putting a structure in place that allows you to develop skill sets that are conducive to success. The daily investment in the right growth initiatives is critical because it will allow you to expand your knowledge, increase your focus, and maximize energy levels. These benefits alone would make the investment in the process worthwhile. However, there is another benefit that comes with the implementation of an effective growth system. When you learn to follow through on your intentions on a consistent daily basis, you are logging key repetitions that allow you to improve your self-discipline. Do not underestimate the importance of this concept. Self-discipline, and the ability to follow through on your intentions, is a foundational pre-requisite to success because it empowers you to get high priority initiatives done even when you don't feel like doing them. Thus, as you start to invest in a growth system, remind yourself to embrace daily doses of discipline so you can cultivate a mindset that will allow you to achieve anything you choose in the future.

Get Back on Track When You Slip Up

It is important to point out that the development of strong self-discipline is a difficult process. Each of us have heard the saying "if it was easy, everyone would do it," and this is 100 percent true when it comes to making things happen on a daily basis. It will be challenging to get up early before the sun is up, when you are still tired and your bed is warm and cozy. There will be many instances where you just want to keep sleeping rather than get up and go through your morning growth routine. These are the times when you earn the right to live your dreams. Don't allow yourself to fall into the trap of listening to your mind when it is telling you to hit the snooze button. Instead, immediately redirect it to what you want to accomplish in your life and jump out of bed to pursue it. Remind yourself that this is a repetition that is required to reach your full potential. In the instances where you hit the snooze button and fall short of expectations, do not make the mistake of beating yourself up and dwelling on it. Simply acknowledge where you fell short and re-commit to making things right as soon as possible. If you are tired of the status quo, then you need to commit to getting back on track every time you slip up.

Don't Expect Immediate Miracles

When it comes to a growth system (or success in general), one of the reasons why so many people fail to follow through on their intentions is that they expect things to come easily. These are individuals who claim to really want to lose weight, but would like it to come with very little mental effort while still eating their favorite dessert on a daily basis. Or it may involve someone who likes the idea of getting up early to invest in themselves, but expects it to immediately be easy to get out of bed when the alarm goes off. Regardless of the situation, when easy does not come, they quickly become frustrated and quit before they have had a chance to progress towards their full potential. Don't fall into the trap of being one of those people expecting instant miracles. This will only lead to a life full of disappointment. Instead, get in the habit of expecting to have to earn all of the unique things you want to accomplish in the future. Put yourself in the rare group of high performers that enjoy making daily investments because they differentiate themselves from other people and take them a step closer to realizing their goals. Do things that others are not willing to do so you can live a life that makes you stand out.

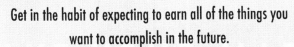

> Get in the habit of expecting to earn all of the things you want to accomplish in the future.
> -@coytecooper

How Was 30-Minutes Ever Too Much?

There is no doubt that the right growth system will drastically transform your life if you make it a habit over an extended period of time. The amount of time to firmly establish the right behaviors varies slightly from one person to the next, but research has shown that habits normally take form in about two months. Because it does vary, there are a couple of signs you can look for to make sure that you have established a sound habit. First, as you invest in the process, it will start to become easier to follow through on your intentions in this area. The one way you can actually be sure that something has become a habit is when it feels unnatural to not follow through on the desired behavior. The second sign will come from an interesting insight that will emerge when you start to realize the tangible benefits that come from your investments. As you reflect on the growth you are experiencing in your life, there will come a moment where you wonder how you ever thought that 30-minutes was too much to invest. Your life will be in a completely different place and the investment in the right habit will be the reason why this is the case. The only thing you need to do now is take action on a desired behavior so you can make this concept a reality for you. Know now that 30-minutes is a small price to pay to transform your life.

FLEXIBILITY IN MORNING ROUTINE

There will be some individuals reading about this "early riser" routine who will not be able to make the morning routine work. It is possible that you are currently on the night shift at work or you may have an infant who makes this routine unproductive. In this case, implement the plan at another time during the day that helps you to maximize momentum. While there are certainly times that have been shown to be more conducive to growth, the most important thing is that you get in the habit of investing in yourself so you can progress towards your aspirations. In terms of the "early riser" routine, if the whole 5:00am thing is a bit much for you, simply start at a later time and progress 15-minutes earlier each week as your body adjusts. Eventually, you will establish this as your habit and getting up will not be an issue. In fact, it is likely that you will even grow to enjoy it because the early time slot is one of the few times in your day when you can work without distractions. On top of this, following through and taking control of your mind in the "battle of the bed" will grow your confidence because you will be demonstrating discipline in an area that is extremely difficult for most people.

GENERATING GROWTH THE REST OF THE DAY

The early morning routine is a good starting point for growth for a variety of different reasons that we have already discussed. With that being said, it is certainly not the only time of the day where you can focus on personal development and growth. In fact, as you progress in developing a system, your mind will be looking for additional times and strategies to compound your efforts. When you have a strong passion for and belief in your vision, you will naturally seek out ways to improve your skill sets so you can eventually live your dreams. There are some natural progressions that are a solid fit for maximizing your personal development. Getting in the habit of taking 5-10 minutes during your lunch hour to revisit your goals and action item steps to make them a reality is a good use of time. In the evening, you can become far more productive by eliminating 30-minutes of television time so you can plan the key activities you will move on the next day. If you still have energy after all that you have done, revisit your goals right before bed so you can activate your subconscious mind to get to work finding ways to achieve your dreams as you sleep.

IMPORTANCE OF REST AND RECOVERY

Humans are meant to be challenged in unique ways. We have been designed in a way where we are most happy when we are stretched beyond our capacities and are moving towards full potential. One of the neatest things about a growth system is that it will ensure that this is taking place on a daily basis. Because it is designed to take you outside of your comfort zone, there will inevitably be times where you feel tired during your day. This will be particularly true when you commit to joining the "5 O'clock Club." The good news is that your body will eventually adjust to this time and you will start to feel energized as you wake up each morning. With that being said, there is also an important need to make sure that you rest and recover when establishing this habit so you can avoid getting burned out and feeling worn down from the process. The key is for you to pay attention to your body and determine if it might be beneficial for you to sleep in on a day or two during the weekend to get a little more rest. Be sure to spend quality time with family and friends so you can recharge to make another push once Monday rolls around. If you learn to take care of your body, it will be more likely to have the energy necessary to follow through on high priority initiatives during the week. The combination of hard work and timely recovery will allow you to realize all of the unique benefits that come with a well-planned growth system.

THE BENEFITS OF GROWTH SYSTEM

The overarching benefit of a growth system is that you are making a commitment to yourself to realize your full potential and to live your best life. This pursuit in itself is something that will bring a sense of accomplishment and excitement as you progress on your journey. If you are not sold on this outcome, then there are several other benefits that will make the commitment worth the investment. Each of these six benefits have the potential to drastically influence your life in ways you may have previously not considered.

1. CRYSTAL CLEAR CLARITY OF VISION. American author Helen Keller explained, "the only thing worse than being blind is having sight but no vision." Legendary scientist and inventor George Washington Carver added, "Where there is no vision there is no hope." There is a reason why vision is so important. If you do not know where you would like to go, then you have no chance of living your purpose and realizing what it is like to live with passion on a daily basis. A growth system maximizes the chances that you will get to do both of these things because it will allow you to cultivate a vision for your life. Once this vision is in place, the structure of a growth system will allow you to focus sharply on proactive thoughts that will help you to stay connected with your aspirations amid life's clutter. So, if you want to live your absolute best life, commit to making sure you have a crystal clear vision. A growth system is a critical step to making sure this becomes a reality in the pursuit to live your dreams.

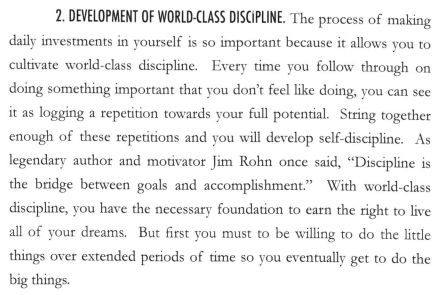

> The only thing worse than being blind is
> having sight but no vision.
> -Helen Keller

2. DEVELOPMENT OF WORLD-CLASS DISCIPLINE. The process of making daily investments in yourself is so important because it allows you to cultivate world-class discipline. Every time you follow through on doing something important that you don't feel like doing, you can see it as logging a repetition towards your full potential. String together enough of these repetitions and you will develop self-discipline. As legendary author and motivator Jim Rohn once said, "Discipline is the bridge between goals and accomplishment." With world-class discipline, you have the necessary foundation to earn the right to live all of your dreams. But first you must to be willing to do the little things over extended periods of time so you eventually get to do the big things.

3. CONFIDENCE IN EARNING RIGHT TO LIVE DREAMS. Before you can accomplish great things, you have to earn the right to do so. One element that is often overlooked is the mental preparation that must occur to perform at a high level. This is why Alexander Graham Bell, who is credited with inventing the first telephone, said "Before anything else, preparation is the key to success." If you are going to perform at a high level, you must cultivate a mindset that is conducive to success. Your growth system will ensure that you get the repetitions necessary to believe that you deserve to achieve great things. As you make investments, your efforts will compound and your confidence will soar. This confidence will lead you to places that you have never gone before and that you previously never considered possible.

> **Before anything else, preparation is the key to success.**
> -Alexander Graham Bell

4. CULTIVATION OF HIGH PERFORMANCE SKILL SETS. When you set unreasonable dreams in your life, they will almost always present you with challenges that you are not currently prepared to conquer. This is perfectly normal as you have set a lofty vision that requires you to get out of your comfort zone to achieve it. In fact, there are likely skill sets that you will need to develop if you are going to be successful in your pursuit. This is where your growth system comes into play. You don't have to cultivate them over night or in the next month, but you need to take steps every single day so that they develop over time. Each morning when you get up, you have an opportunity to put in a repetition to develop these skill sets. With a proactive approach and enough repetitions, it is inevitable that these will progressively turn in to extraordinary skill sets that will allow you to perform at a high level in the pursuit of your dreams.

5. ABILITY TO DEAL WITH DAILY CHALLENGES. Most people structure their schedule so they can get as much sleep as possible before they start their day. This often involves waking up 30-minutes before they are supposed to be out the door and rushing to make sure they are to work on time. This could take a variety of different forms depending on a person's situation in life, but the point is that they allow sleep to dictate their overall approach to their day. As a result, there has been no time given to mentally prepare for the challenges that are presented on a daily basis. This often leads to poor decisions because your mind is rushed and is not prepared to make sound judgment calls. The morning routine allows you to set the pace for your day and to ensure that your mind is in a productive place when you head to work. By starting your day with activities that are productive in nature, your mind naturally learns to look for the positive and this allows you to get off to a great start. On top of this, by revisiting goals and values, you stay focused on the things that are most important and this ultimately helps improve your decision-making throughout the day.

6. BECOME THE EXACT PERSON YOU WANT TO BE. Few people take the time to know exactly what they would like to achieve in life, or who they would like to become as a person. As a result, they often float from one day to the next and simply take what life gives them. More often than not, life gives them something that is far from their full potential. The investment in your morning routine starts a process that will allow you to know exactly where you would like to go in life. By reading the right books and reflecting on your inner thoughts, you give yourself a chance to truly understand what you value the most and what you would like to achieve in life. This will ensure that you tap into a passion that will energize and guide your actions on a daily basis. All you have to do to start this process is get up early and invest 30-minutes in a growth routine. Eventually, your efforts will compound and you will be glad you made the investment.

"You don't have to be great to get started, but you have
to get started to be great."
-@LesBrown77

Take Action Today

Even the best of intentions will alone do nothing to change your life if you do not learn to follow through. In the words of motivational speaker Les Brown, "You don't have to be great to get started, but you have to get started to be great." The world is full of people with lost dreams because they have failed to take action in their life. If you want to realize full potential and live your best life, then you need to take action on one thing today that will allow you to start building momentum. You do not need to have all the answers on how you are going to achieve all of your dreams. But you must stop thinking so much and instead start doing. Commit to getting up tomorrow 30 minutes early and reading a motivational book (preferably this one) that energizes you as you start your day. Even if you don't feel like it when the alarm goes off, remind yourself that you have to earn the right to live your dreams and do it anyway. As you win the "battle of the bed" day after day, you will get the repetitions necessary to build your self-discipline and your confidence will soar.

Eventually, this will allow you to reap all the benefits associated with investing in a morning routine and you will be inspired to add other growth elements that can transform your life. It is at this point where all kinds of great things will happen in your life because your mind will be in a proactive state that is characterized by abundance. You will have built a mindset where you truly believe you deserve success and this will guide you in pursuing a new vision that is far beyond anything you previously thought possible. However, before you are ready for this, we need to touch on creating the vision, values, and victories necessary to live an extraordinary life.

> **The best of intentions will alone do nothing to change your life if you do not learn to follow through.**
>
> -@coytecooper

JOHN MAXWELL

Dr. John Maxwell is one of the premier experts in the world on leadership and personal development. Throughout his career, he has made a drastic impact on the world through his different growth initiatives designed to add value to people. These include EQUIP and the John Maxwell Company which have trained over five million leaders worldwide. On top of this, he has sold over 20 million books and is an international speaker that delivers uplifting messages across the world. So, what makes Dr. Maxwell so effective? One of the things that he believes crafted his success was the investment in a growth plan early in his career as a pastor. Realizing he was limited in his leadership by his current skill sets, he committed to a growth plan that would stretch his abilities and has never looked back. In addition to creating detailed plans to maximize growth, Dr. Maxwell has become well known for his ability to reflect and identify areas of improvement in his life on a consistent basis. One specific example is his routine over the holidays. After Christmas, he sets aside an entire week to assess his performance for the previous year. He is able to do this because he keeps a detailed calendar of the previous 12 months so he knows exactly how he is spending his time. With this information, he examines potential areas of growth and how he can spend his time more efficiently in the upcoming new year to reach full potential. It is this proactive approach to growth that has made him an amazing difference maker in people's lives and that has allowed him to make a lasting impact on the world.

KEY SUMMARY POINTS

O   Success is not something that happens by accident. The most successful people in the world invest in a daily structure that allows them to maximize growth and to be as efficient as possible.

O   A simple morning routine consisting of reading the right books, journaling, and revisiting your goals can drastically transform your life if you have the discipline to implement it on a daily basis.

O   You will slip up at times when you are implementing a growth system. In these times, get back on track as quickly as possible and commit to making them a habit so you can realize full potential.

O   There are six unique benefits that are associated with a solid growth system. These benefits are essential elements for reaching full potential and living your best life.

1. Crystal clear clarity of vision
2. Development of world-class discipline
3. Confidence in earning right to live dreams
4. Cultivation of elite performance skill sets
5. Ability to deal with daily challenges
6. Become the exact person you want to be

S INEVITABLE. PURSUE THE THING YOU ARE MEANT TO DO ALL OUT AND MAKING YOUR MARK IS INEVITABLE. PURS

CHAPTER 4

ACHIEVE CRYSTAL CLEAR CLARITY IN YOUR VISION

> " There is one quality one must possess to win, and that is the definiteness of purpose, the knowledge of what one wants, and a burning desire to possess it. To accomplish this requires practical dreamers who can, and will, put their dreams into action. "
>
> -Napoleon Hill

ONE OF THE most powerful attributes in the entire world for any individual is a certainty of knowing exactly what they want to achieve in life. When a person has cultivated a fully committed mindset to realize their purpose, they experience a clarity that allows them to know exactly how they want to live each day. On top of this, they have a unique energy that drives them because they understand the reason why they were put on this earth. It is also something that breeds high performance because they have acquired the one quality mentioned by *Think and Grow Rich* author Napoleon Hill. They have a definiteness of purpose that allows them to understand the knowledge they want to acquire and the burning desire to achieve it. Yet this quality of understanding the definiteness of purpose is something that eludes most people because life is filled with clutter that distracts us on a daily basis. Most people never have the chance to live to full potential simply because they do not carve out the time necessary to determine the exact life they would like to live. Thus, they tend to float from one day to the next without any direction because they are not in touch with their vision or values. This is not how you were created to live. You are meant to live with a desire to achieve something truly unique. This is exactly why you need to have the self-discipline to take the time to begin with the end in mind.

 You are meant to live with a desire to achieve something truly unique.
-@coytecooper

Begin With The End In Mind

In Dr. Stephen Covey's iconic best-selling book *The 7 Habits of Highly Effective People*, he discusses the concept of beginning with the end in mind. In simple terms, he explains that you must create a picture of the things you would like to accomplish in your life first in your mind so you have an opportunity to make them a reality in your physical life. This is reinforced in his concept that "all things are created twice." For lofty aspirations, there is a first creation in your mind that acts as a blue print to help guide your efforts on a day-to-day basis. Eventually, when you act on making this blue print a reality consistently over time, it allows for what Dr. Covey refers to as the second creation to occur in your physical world. In essence, this is when you get the chance to realize the picture you first created in your mind in your actual real life.

Basic Breakdown of Vision

The previous "begin with the end in mind" concept by Dr.

Stephen Covey is an ideal portrayal of vision. It encompasses the ability to visualize the things that you would like to achieve in your mind. The starting point for this process is simply making the decision that you would like to have a specific vision that guides you on a day-to-day basis in your life. At this point, you should also start to train your mind to look beyond normal expectations. It is important that you break down any limitations that your mind has been trained to believe when it comes to what you can achieve. This is an essential step because it will allow your mind to run wild dreaming about your future and exactly how you would like it to play out. If you could live any life you wanted, what would that life look like? Assuming you could not fail, what are the things that you would pursue with a passion to make a part of your life? These are the types of things that you can and should consider when approaching your long-term planning process. To simplify things, go through the following three questions that relate to your aspirations in the future:

1. Who do you want to become someday as a person?
2. What would you like to have in your life?
3. What would you like to accomplish?

If you have never seriously considered these questions, there is a good chance that your answers will be a little unclear as you get started. This is a normal response and you need to remind yourself that this is just a starting point for the creation of your vision. Continue to ask yourself these three questions until you have some initial answers that inspire you to take action outside of your comfort zone. Once you have some outcomes that energize you, it is time to start visualizing these accomplishments in your mind so you activate your subconscious brain. When you engage in this process and create an initial picture of your aspirations in your mind, it will provide your subconscious brain with a blue print of your vision so it can get to work finding ways to make it a reality in the future.

> That some achieve great success, is proof to all that others can achieve it as well.
> -Abraham Lincoln

GETTING PERMISSION TO PURSUE YOUR DREAMS

At some point, we have all been told that we are not good enough or that we should tone down our aspirations because they are too lofty. If it was not said, then it was inferred and it had the same impact on you. It caused you to question your ability to achieve your aspirations and eventually these types of thoughts may have resulted in you abandoning pursuing your dreams altogether. Let's clear something up right now. It was wrong for these people to do this to you and they should not have done it. However, it is also time to stop allowing people to dictate what you can accomplish in life. You do not need anyone's permission to pursue your dreams and it is time for you to start taking full responsibility for the exact life you will have in the future. This starts by acknowledging that you have complete control of your thoughts and actions every single day. Start by committing to the elimination of negative thoughts that limit your potential and instead focus on creating a vision that allows you to live a remarkable life. If you are brave enough to believe you can achieve extraordinary things, you immediately differentiate yourself from the 97 percent of people who settle for the status quo. Instead, you place yourself in a position to soar with the three percent of high performers who go on to achieve their dreams. Why can't you live the exact life that you envision in your mind? When you break down the elements of what would make this life possible, it is almost certain that someone else has already shown that it is possible. In the words of the great United States' President Abraham Lincoln, "That some achieve great success, is proof to all that others can achieve it as well."

IF RUSS CAN DO IT, THEN WHY NOT YOU?

If you follow the National Football League (NFL), then you have likely heard the name Russell Wilson. While he has started to establish himself as one of the premier quarterbacks in the NFL, his outlook as a professional football player was not always promising in the eyes of scouts and analysts. At 5 foot 11 inches and 200 pounds, he was said to be too short to see his receivers and too small to take the hits because of his scrambling style of play. The good news for Russell is that he did not have to listen to this criticism because he believed he had every right to pursue his dream. And that is exactly what he did as he became an integral part of the 2014 Seattle Seahawks Super Bowl championship team.

When asked about how his mental approach and his belief in his ability to play in the NFL, he said his dad always asked him "Russ, why not you?" when discussing aspirations. In response, Russell has created a mantra that has inspired both his team and others to pursue their highest potential. It reads "Why not me? Why not you? Why not us? Why not now? Why not again? Why not try?" If Russell Wilson can defy the odds and become an elite quarterback in the NFL, then there is every reason to believe that you can live out your dreams if you believe in your ability to do so. With a clear vision and a passion to be great, you have every right to live your best life. Why not you?

> " Why not me? Why not you? Why not us? Why not now? Why not again? Why not try? "
> -@DangeRussWilson

Believing in Your Ability to Achieve It

If there is one thing that all extraordinary achievers have in common, it is that they have a crstyal clear vision and confidence in their ability to achieve it. This is an absolute pre-requisite if you are going to perform at a high level and make your mark on the world. American philosopher and psychologist William James explained this about this mindset: "Our belief at the beginning of a doubtful undertaking is the one thing that assures the successful outcome of any adventure." There are few pieces of literature that better illustrate this point than the famous poem *Thinking* by Walter D. Wintle that emphasizes the importance of belief:

> If you think you are beaten, you are
> If you think you dare not, you don't,
> If you like to win, but you think you can't
> It is almost certain you won't.
>
> If you think you'll lose, you've lost
> For out of the world we find,
> Success begins with a fellow's will
> It's all in the state of mind.
>
> If you think you are outclassed, you are
> You've got to think high to rise,
> You've got to be sure of yourself before
> You can ever win a prize.
>
> Life's battles don't always go
> To the stronger or faster man,
> But soon or late the man who wins
> Is the man WHO THINKS HE CAN!

It is so important that you believe in your ability to achieve your dreams. This is what it will take to realize your vision so get to work each day putting in the repetitions to earn it. Eventually, the consistency in your investments will pay off as you will build confidence that will allow you to achieve remarkable accomplishments.

CLEARING THE CLUTTER TO MEET VISION

While the purpose of this chapter is to encourage you to pursue your vision, there is value in considering why this pursuit does not end up working out for everyone. We have already touched on the fact that life's busyness makes it extremely challenging to focus in on any one area at a given time. This is particularly true with the evolution of technology and all of the different stimuli that demand our attention on a daily basis. This is all referred to as "clutter" and it can pull you away from your purpose and vision if you are not disciplined with your daily approach. This is one of the main reasons why many adults have no clear vision of the things they would like to accomplish in their life. They simply do not have time to focus on the things that truly matter to them. Or at least this is what they tell themselves.

The truth is that it is always within your power to clear the clutter at any moment so you can create time to explore and pursue the things you are passionate about. But you must have the self-discipline to commit to making the time necessary to explore your vision. It is the only real way that you will eventually get to the point where you are pursuing aspirations that energize you on a daily basis. If you want to live a life that you are excited about each morning and that gives you a feeling of purpose, take the time to clear the clutter so you eventually have the opportunity to meet your vision.

THE EVOLUTION OF VISION

Once you have cleared the clutter and started to ask yourself questions about where you would like to go with your life, you have begun the process of cultivating a vision that will guide you moving forward. It is in the very early stages, but it is a start that you must have to realize your full potential. This is the point where your mind starts to become engaged again and thoughts take form that can drastically change your life. After all, as explained by author and poet Oliver Wendell Holmes, "One's mind, once stretched by a new idea, never regains its original dimensions." Simply taking the steps to realize your vision can put into motion a series of actions that will change your mind forever. This all starts with the seed of a single thought that you have about living your best life. My hope is that this book will provide you with the seed thoughts that will drastically transform your life as you go all out to pursue your dreams.

One's mind, once stretched by a new idea, never regains its original dimensions.

-Oliver Wendell Holmes

THE SEED OF A SINGLE IDEA

It is an empowering concept to consider that all amazing accomplishments in this world germinated within someone's mind in the form of a single thought. They were simply an idea that flashed into the mind of someone who was smart enough to recognize it and then take steps to put that idea into action. While this sounds pretty fundamental, it is something that is actually quite difficult and achieved only by high performers. The reason for this is because great ideas can be both difficult to cultivate and hard to recognize. You must first train your mind to think creatively so you can cultivate ideas that will tap into your energy and areas of genius. The challenge is that most people struggle with thinking outside the box because they have listened to other's criticism all their life and have conformed to thoughts that are more consistent with the status quo. The good news is that you can start to change this immediately by investing in a growth system that develops your mind. When your brain is constantly exposed to the right types of materials, eventually it will put things together and you will start to cultivate thoughts capable of taking your life to an entirely new level. As you stretch your mind, it will take a new form and you will expand your ability to cultivate and recognize extraordinary ideas. If you are skeptical about this concept, consider this quote by the legendary Apple founder Steve Jobs: "Creativity is just connecting things. When you ask creative people how they did something, they feel a little guilty because they didn't really do it, they just saw something. It seemed obvious to them after a while. That's because they were able to connect experiences they've had and synthesize new things."

Even when your mind produces these creative thoughts more regularly, it is important that you take things a step further than recognizing them. After all, a great idea in someone's mind does absolutely no good if it just stays there and does not have an opportunity to branch out. In fact, if you do not make a habit of acting on these intuitions, it is likely that they will disappear from your mind and you will lose them forever. It is useful for you to learn to see each one of these ideas as seeds that have the potential to grow into something unique. Once you are confident you have a seed that can become something truly remarkable, then you need to commit to planting it by taking immediate action to make it a reality in the physical world. In the early stages, it is likely that your vision for these ideas will be cloudy because you will not have had the chance to learn from repetition that comes from pursuing your dreams. As you implement your ideas and embrace the process, you will have an opportunity to learn from repetition and your vision will eventually become crystal clear in your mind.

Forecast From Cloudy to Clear

Picture a morning where you wake up and your surroundings are so caked with fog that you are only able to see 20 feet in front of you. This is likely how your vision will be when you start this process. You will not be sure exactly where you want your life to go and the dreams that you have initially set will be foggy at best. However, as you invest in the growth process, the fog will start to lift and eventually it will be like an overcast day with periods where the sun peeks through. In moments like these, fishermen in Alaska can see for miles because these brief moments of sunlight force their way through the clouds and illuminate the landscape. Similarly, when it comes to your vision, there will be instances like these so-called moments of clarity where you are able to see your dreams with a crystal clear picture in your mind. However, just like an overcast day, these will flash out of your mind and you will be left with a cloudy picture of where you want to travel with your life in the future. The good news with vision is that it can be far more predictable than weather. That is, you will have more control over the outlook and clarity if you invest in an approach that keeps you connected to your vision. If you are not convinced that investing in a clear vision is worth your attention, it would be wise to consider some of the benefits that come from knowing exactly where you would like to travel in the future.

Benefits of a "Crystal Clear" Vision

The most powerful benefit that comes with a crystal clear vision is knowing with certainty the exact life you hope to live in the future. This is a life altering insight because it provides you with an end destination where you can focus your full attention in the pursuit to make it a reality. In Brian Tracy's *Goals! How to Get Everything You Want - Faster Than You Ever Thought Possible*, he discusses homing pigeons and how they have the unique ability to return to their home even if you take them thousands of miles away in any direction. He goes on to say that humans have this same ability when they are absolutely clear about where they would like to go in life. Here is what is really cool about a crystal clear vision when you activate your homing potential. No matter what life throws at you, it will not matter because you will naturally continue to move progressively towards your vision. That is, when you invest in a system where you make it a daily habit to stay focused on your vision. When you achieve and reinforce clarity in a meaningful direction for your life, it immediately instills a formidable energy into your body because you are connecting with your purpose. It will be as if you are unleashing an unstoppable inner desire that has been buried deep down inside you waiting to be released.

On top of instilling energy and purpose into your life, the ability to get clear with your vision will allow you to become far more efficient in making effective decisions to pursue your dreams and goals. It is an empowering feeling to know exactly what you are supposed to pursue on a daily basis and it makes it far easier to say no to things that do not advance your vision. In fact, the moment your vision becomes crystal clear, you will feel obligated to say no to good opportunities because you will know that this is the only way you will eventually get the chance to live your dreams. This ability is important because it will clear your schedule so you can narrow in on the pursuit of your vision with laser-like precision. All of this will result in a calmness in your state of mind because you will be pursuing the exact life you know you should be living.

How to Create a "Crystal Clear" Vision

For most people, it is not possible to achieve a crystal clear vision in a few short sessions. It is more likely that it will be the result of consistent investments over time because clarity in your vision is something that takes significant inner work and reflection. The good news is that we have already touched on early steps you can take to make this a reality in the previous chapter on the implementation of a growth system. The morning routine alone will go a long way in helping this come to fruition because it involves investing in yourself and getting your mind in a proactive state to pursue your passions. However, in the meantime, there are additional activities you should consider that will help you flush out an initial vision. It is important that you are patient with yourself during this process because it will likely take you time and a series of revisions until you have a vision that is worthy of your full attention. If you continue to invest in the process, eventually your long-term aspirations will emerge and you will reap all the benefits that come from a crystal clear vision. We will explore five steps you can take to make this a reality in your life.

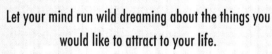

> Let your mind run wild dreaming about the things you would like to attract to your life.
>
> -@coytecooper

1. CREATE A "DREAM LIST". Now that you have committed to a growth system, one of the first things you can do as you journal is to start a "dream list" of all the things you would like to accomplish in your life. This is the starting point for determining the vision that will guide all of your efforts in the future. To make this happen, sit down with a pen and a piece of paper and simply jot down things that you would absolutely pursue if failure were not an option. At this point, don't worry at all about how you are going to achieve them because this will come at a later time. Simply let your mind run wild dreaming about the things you would like to attract to your life. While it is your choice on how to create the list, it is always good to have a balance of personal and professional dream items. On the personal side, you might dream of having a family and being able to travel the world with them. On the professional side, it might energize you to think of starting a company that impacts people in your community and state. This might even include material items that you would like to earn. There are no limits to the things that you list here as long as they will add real value to your life. Once you have a list you are excited about, move on and make sure they pass the "Unreasonable Reality Check."

2. PERFORM "UNREASONABLE" REALITY CHECK. You have been taught to be reasonable in your expectations most of your life. We are not going to do that here. In fact, as you look through your list, I want you to ask the question of whether other people would think your expectations are unreasonable. If the answer is "no" to many of your dreams, then you are probably not setting high enough standards. If this is the case, then go back and push yourself to consider another level that makes you uncomfortable. Choose things that you are not capable of achieving in the immediate future because you lack the skill sets to make them a reality. This will force you to get out of your comfort zone to acquire these skill sets. When you can answer "yes" to the "Unreasonable Reality Check" test, then you are ready to move on to the next step. Make it your priority to set standards that will inspire others as they come to fruition.

3. TEACH THAT LITTLE VOICE TO SHUT UP. Whenever you set lofty aspirations, the world is required to test how much you truly want to achieve your goals by placing obstacles in front of you. This can come in the form of adversity where you get knocked flat on your back and fall way short of expectations or it may be the criticism from others that tell you that you are not capable of achieving your dreams. It may even be a brief moment where you stop and wonder if your dreams are too much. It is in these moments where you need to tell the little voice in the back of your mind encouraging you to quit to shut up. It is your ability to redirect your mind back to the bigger picture when facing obstacles that will determine whether or not you get to live your dreams. Win the battle over that little voice so that you have the confidence to realize your full potential.

4. PRIORITIZE YOUR DREAMS. Once you create a list of dreams that have passed the "Unreasonable Reality Check," it is important to take the time to prioritize your list. The reality is that not all of your dreams will have the same level of importance and you need to take the time to comprehend this so you know how to dedicate your time moving forward. It will also guide you as you narrow in on shorter-term goals and daily action item checklists. While prioritizing can be an extremely difficult task, as you are differentiating between outcomes you are passionate about, it is essential because it will allow you to de-clutter your life. In this exercise, you should focus on identifying 2-3 top tier dreams that you plan to pursue with your full attention. Even with these top tier dreams, it is important that you order them so you know how to proceed with your efforts. The good news is that if you choose the right dreams, it will likely contribute to the achievement of the other dreams you have on your list. This will absolutely be true when you have taken the time to ask the "why" question when considering your aspirations. This is a process that may inspire you to revisit your dreams so you can refine your list. The key is to have alignment in your vision and dreams so there is no confusion in your approach.

5. ASK THE "WHY" QUESTION. The tricky thing about the early phase of setting dreams is that they are often influenced by our past experiences. While this is not always a bad thing, it is important to recognize that these influences could mean that you are choosing things that are not actually your dreams. It is possible that they are your parents' because of their constant pursuit to push you to live a certain type of life. The point is that lofty, "unreasonable" dreams are so difficult that you must be ready to go all in to make them a reality. You cannot do this if they are not something you are truly passionate about. To help flush this out, move through each of the items in your dream list and ask yourself why you want to achieve them. If you were to make them a reality, what would it add to your life that would make it a worthwhile investment? If your "why" is something that seems noble and energizes you, then you have likely picked something that is worth pursuing every single day with full potential for however long it takes. The ability to determine the "why" for each of your dreams will also go a long way in helping you to determine your vision. The key is identifying trends in the dreams that fill your body with excitement and inspiration when you think about achieving them. This will give you clues on what you are meant to do with your life. It will at least give you a starting point.

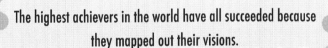

> The highest achievers in the world have all succeeded because they mapped out their visions.
> -@DarrenHardy

WHY ASK WHY?

In *Start With Why*, best selling author Simon Sinek outlines a central component for all extraordinary achievements. Regardless of whether it is an organization, team, or individual, the one thing that they have in common is that they start with a why that inspires them to pursue excellence. Whether it be organizations like Disney and Southwest Airlines or individuals like John F. Kennedy or Ronald Reagan, they are all clear as to the exact reason why they are pursuing lofty ambitions. It is this clarity that keeps them focused on a daily basis among life's clutter and motivated when facing adversity that comes during their journey. Best selling author of *The Compound Effect* Darren Hardy explains the criticality of focusing on a vision with a strong why: "Something almost magical happens when you organize and focus your creative power on a well-defined target. I've seen this time and again: the highest achievers in the world have all succeeded because they mapped out their visions. The person who has a clear, compelling, and white-hot burning why will always defeat even the best of the best at doing the how." The key is to have a compelling enough why so that you will continue to pursue your vision when things get challenging and life tests your resolve.

Transitioning "Why" to Concrete Vision

When you ask the "why" question often enough, you will eventually come up with a list of aspirations that you are inspired to achieve. These cumulative aspirations, when connected with a common underlying theme, become your vision. It is the culminating picture that you have for your life that includes the things you would like to have, what you would like to accomplish, and the person you would like to become. When this vision includes noble pursuits, it is inevitable that it will spark an energy inside you that changes the way you approach your day. If this does not happen, then I suggest that you reassess your responses to make sure that they are not dominated by superficial aspirations that are the result of your ego. The burning desire to pursue your best life comes when you are pursuing a higher calling that impacts the lives of others in some unique way. This is what Napoleon Hill referred to at the start of the chapter. It is your purpose, what you were put on this earth to do, and when you know exactly what this is, it will drastically transform the way you interact with life. When this vision becomes clear, you will do whatever is necessary in a productive manner to make it happen. This is the core foundation of all extraordinary accomplishments and it is something that you should pursue with your full attention until it becomes a reality for you.

THERE ARE NO GUARANTEES

Few things in life are guaranteed. The process of laying out a clear vision that is connected to your purpose is no different. It does not guarantee that you will achieve all the exact dreams you have for your life. In fact, without intentional action to make your blue print a reality, it is more likely that you will never get the chance to bring them to fruition in your physical world. However, if you take immediate action towards your dreams and cultivate a desire to achieve them, you drastically increase your chances to realize your vision. But there still are no guarantees! You want to know why? Because there is no guarantee you won't go out and completely blow your own mind as you perform beyond your expectations. It is possible that you will grow so much that your initial vision will morph into something with the potential to make an extraordinary impact on the world. There simply are no guarantees when it comes to vision. It may not end up being exactly what you thought it would be, but it may also end up being something far better than you ever initially imagined.

> There is no guarantee you won't go out and completely blow your own mind as you perform beyond your expectations.
> -@coytecooper

WELL, EXCEPT FOR THIS ONE THING...

Remember when I said that there were no guarantees when it comes to vision? Well, I was wrong because there is one thing that the pursuit of your dreams will guarantee. When you invest in the right daily approach, it is absolutely inevitable that you will grow and take steps towards realizing your full potential. There is no question that stepping outside of your comfort zone and pursuing your best life will allow you to be better. This is one thing that you can always control regardless of what is going on in your external environment. This is the beauty of being bold and pursuing your dreams. They are seeds that emerge in your mind and once you act upon them, your mind evolves and it is never the same. When you get in the habit of pursuing them with a passion every single day, eventually your brain will mature to the point where it is capable of extraordinary things that leave a lasting mark on the world.

THE JOURNEY STARTS NOW

If you have not started the journey to pursue your vision, then the best time to start is now. It is a process that will take time to get in place so it is important that you invest in immediate steps to live your best life and to achieve great things. The one thing that is important for you to understand is that you do not need to know all the answers right now on how to make it happen. It would be impossible for you to know exactly how to make it a reality because creating a crystal clear vision is a process that is unique to each person and it is only achieved by those who invest in the personal development process. It is important that you get comfortable with initially not knowing all the answers and instead focus on implementing a daily process that allows you to consistently grow. The time will come where you will know, but it is not likely that it will be today. Don't let this scare you off. Embrace uncertainty as a critical part of the journey that you must conquer to live your best life.

You Will Just Know!!!

The question people often pose when discussing vision is "how will I know when I have found it?" While often not what they want to hear, my response is always "YOU WILL JUST KNOW!!!" When you have earned it through consistent growth and reflection over time, your vision will emerge from the clouds and become clear to you. When this moment arrives, you will know what you were put on this earth to do. Thomas Edison knew that he was meant to invent and create things that would change the world forever. Once he knew this, there was nothing that was going to stop him from making his mental vision a reality in the physical world. When he failed over 10,000 times, his energy to innovative did not waiver because he was crystal clear on what he wanted to achieve. This clarity, this desire is what led him to be one of the greatest inventors of all-time. My hope is that your journey allows you to eventually know what it is like to have this kind of passion. One that drives you to make your mark on the world even when facing extreme challenges. There is something deep inside you, but nobody can find it but you. The ball is in your court.

THE MAKE YOUR MARK MASTER

HOWARD SCHULTZ

When you hear the word coffee, many people in the United States quickly associate the word with Starbucks. The company has become a household name, but this was not always the case. In fact, Starbucks started with modest beginnings that included a few retail stores in the Seattle area. Howard Schultz, hired to manage the retail stores, visited Italy and was inspired with a vision to make Starbucks into a staple of everyday culture in America where getting coffee was what you just did. Unfortunately, the then owners of Starbucks disagreed with his assessment as their initial business model was more geared towards retail sales. Undeterred, Schultz left the company and started his first coffee shop in Seattle in 1986. He proceeded to open an additional two that were highly successful before purchasing the Starbucks company to establish it as his primary brand. This crystal clear vision has led to Starbucks to being a worldwide entity with 21,000 stores in 65 countries. In many areas across the world, Schultz has succeeded at making coffee and Starbucks a part of the every day culture.

KEY SUMMARY POINTS

○   You can put yourself in the top 3 percent of high performers by writing down your dreams/goals and revisiting them on a daily basis.

○   All great accomplishments start as a single idea in someone's mind. However, successful people take steps to recognize these ideas and make them a reality.

○   Clarity in vision will provide you with unique benefits that will transform your life. However, you must be willing to work at personal development and reflection over time to earn the right to have a crystal clear vision.

○   When your "why" is strong enough, you will do what it takes to make your vision a reality. Spend the time to make sure that you have a strong "why" connected to your long-term aspirations.

CHAPTER 5

GIVE YOURSELF THE GREATEST GIFT OF ALL AND SET GOALS

" Setting goals is the first step in turning the invisible into visible.
-Anthony Robbins "

THE PROCESS OF turning your vision into a reality all starts when you develop the ability to set goals that guide your daily actions. We already know that vision provides you with an initial blueprint of where you would like to go in life. It is the detailed, long-term picture of the exact life you hope to live in the future. For all intents and purposes, this vision is something that is invisible in your physical world. Because of the fact that it is a distant reality in your mind, vision can sometimes be overwhelming if you don't learn to start closing the gap on it immediately. This is exactly where goals come in to play. They are the shorter-term aspirations that provide a structure for progressing towards your vision when they are implemented correctly. From a planning standpoint, they are actually very similar to dreams in their overall purpose and potential impact on your life. In simple terms, they should guide your daily actions by keeping you focused on an end destination that you plan to pursue with your full attention on a daily basis. The primary difference with goals is that they are generally shorter term and they have specific criteria you must consider for them to be successful. Before we touch on these criteria, we will discuss the basic concept of goals and how they can transform your life.

GOAL SETTING 101

Goal setting is the process of outlining specific outcomes that we would like to achieve in the somewhat near future. For the purposes of this process, we will call this somewhat near future within the next five years. However, we will focus sharply on one-year goals as the standard in this chapter because they are absolutely essential to success when it comes to pursuing your vision and living your best life. They are far enough out that they force you to stretch outside of your comfort zone to achieve them, but not so far out that they are difficult to envision and implement into your life. In addition, they are an ideal starting point because their scope allows you to identify action items you can take on a daily basis to help make them a reality.

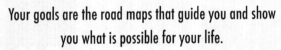

> Your goals are the road maps that guide you and show
> you what is possible for your life.
> -@LesBrown77

It is essential that you get the chance to experience these key elements so you can fully grasp the impact that goals can have on your life. In more general terms, goals are essential to success because they give you something specific to pursue with your full potential each day. While most people are floating in their day-to-day approach, you will have the opportunity to move with purpose because you will have no confusion as to what is most important to you in your life. This is an empowering moment because it will make it far more likely that you are able to say no to things that are counterproductive to your success. This will allow you to become far more efficient in focusing your attention on initiatives that will move you directly towards your goals.

THE BRAIN'S CENTRAL NAVIGATION SYSTEM

The brain is a magnificent tool that can take us extraordinary places, but it cannot do this unless we tell it exactly where to go. This is where goals come in to play. The moment you set quality goals and commit to pursuing them, it provides your brain with a set direction to travel. As explained by speaker Les Brown, "Your goals are the road maps that guide you and show you what is possible for your life." It is as if you are planning a long trip and punched the end destination into a navigation system that has the capability to take you to your desired location. The brain has this same unique ability, but you must continually revisit your goals until they have been communicated clearly to your subconscious brain. Eventually, your subconscious brain will sort through all the clutter of information that it receives and acknowledge your goal as an essential destination. When this happens, it will dedicate its massive capacity to creating a path to make the outcome a reality. However, it is important to comprehend that you must take action towards your initial list of goals to make this process happen. Once the goal is firmly imprinted into your subconscious mind, you will be ready to make your first trip on the journey to realize your vision. That is, if you have chosen goals that are in alignment with your long-term aspirations in life.

MAPPING OUT DESTINATION CHECKPOINTS

Given the amazing navigation capabilities of the brain, it makes sense that you would include your entire long-term plan in the input process. If your end destination is your vision, then it is critical that you revisit the things you are passionate about achieving someday so they are crystal clear to your subconscious brain. This will provide your brain with the absolute end outcome of where you hope to eventually arrive through your efforts. Once you have done this, it is important to input destination checkpoints that will allow you to proceed towards your vision. This is where your goals come in to play because they are designed to serve as progression points in your trip to live your dreams. If you set goals that do not meet this requirement, they may energize you temporarily when you achieve them, but you will end up feeling disappointed and/or frustrated because they are not contributing to the primary reason why you were put on this earth. It is important that you set goals with your vision in mind so they serve as check points on your way to achieving extraordinary things and living your best life.

Goal Setting Is a Gift

The first thing for you to understand about goals is that they are a gift that you can give to yourself at any time. In fact, they are the greatest gift you can give to yourself because they will allow you to immediately move towards a life that is more in alignment with your full potential. The moment you take the time to know what you are passionate about achieving in the future, a shift takes place in your mind that has the potential to drastically change your entire approach to living. When you are clear about exactly what you hope to achieve, it allows you to make decisions to strategically progress towards your vision with a definite purpose. This will allow you to give yourself the gift of energy and purpose because you will be pursuing your best life and this is ultimately what you were put on this earth to do. Few people ever give themselves this gift because most people do not understand the impact that goals, and the specificity of intentions, can have on their lives. Some people comprehend the importance of goals, but they do not follow through on them because they are not willing to develop the self-discipline to make them a reality. They are too caught up in the clutter that life presents to take the steps necessary to progress towards their vision.

You Cannot Buy The Greatest Gifts

We give ourselves gifts on a regular basis. The problem is that we often give ourselves gifts that do not add real value to our lives. When we shop for materials goods, they often give us a short-term burst of positive energy, but this is not something that lasts. I'm sure each of you can relate. Whether it is a car, house, clothes, or another object you desire, there is an immediate excitement that comes when you purchase the item. However, at some point, the item is no longer new and you eventually lose this feeling of excitement. So, most people continually feel the urge to acquire new things so they can recapture the feeling, and this often leads to a never-ending cycle of pursuing stuff that you think you need. This is a mistake because it will never allow you to feel fulfilled and satisfied in your life on a more permanent basis. The only way to truly earn this feeling is by pursuing initiatives that are in alignment with your vision. This is exactly why goal setting is the best possible gift that you can give yourself. The process will provide you with unique benefits that will drastically transform your life if you have the self-discipline to make it a regular part of your daily routine.

What Gifts Will You Get?

Given that you are human, you are likely asking yourself the questions, "what gifts?" and "how can they impact my life?" These are both great questions and ones that we want to address immediately so you are ready to fully commit to setting goals in your life. The first gift that you would be giving yourself, and that is often the most appealing to people, is the ability to drastically improve performance in key areas. The immediate benefit of setting goals is a sharp focus on something that is important to you and this reallocates your energy towards improving your ability to produce and progress. Regardless of what goal you have chosen, you have the opportunity to be significantly better at what you do on a daily basis. As a result, you are allowed to experience the second gift relating to goal setting that has to do with drastically increasing your chances to realize success. As explained by Earl Nightingale, "People with goals succeed because they know where they are going." This specificity allows them to move with purpose towards noble accomplishments and this results in a life associated with success. And when performed with the larger picture in mind, setting goals allows you to realize the third and fourth gifts of progressing towards your vision and making a difference in the world. In the words of legendary Microsoft founder and humanitarian Bill Gates, "Goals are the key to achieving improvement in the human condition."

> People with goals succeed because they know where they are going.
> -Earl Nightingale

GOALS ARE NOT NEW YEAR'S RESOLUTIONS

Each year, nearly 40 million Americans write down their New Year's resolutions with the hopes that they will transform their lives. The problem is that for most people these are simply hopes and there is no real follow through to make them a reality. This is exactly why research has shown that only 8 percent of people actually follow through on making their resolutions happen. This means that only 3.2 million of the 40 million people that make commitments to change their lives at the start of each year actually realize them! This is a staggering statistic that illustrates the challenge that most people have with following through on their intentions. As we break down goals in this chapter, it is important to remind yourself that this process is not going to be like the New Year's resolution statistic. Refuse to allow yourself to become a statistic that is representative of the people who fail to realize their goals and full potential. Step up and embrace this advice from legendary financier J.P. Morgan: "The first steps towards getting somewhere is to decide that you are not going to stay where you are." If you are not happy with your current situation or if you have much higher aspirations, it is important to commit to taking action immediately so you can live a much more fulfilling life.

If You Are Bored With Life

There are so many people in the world that are unhappy with their current situation. This is in large part because they have not taken the time to know the things that they are passionate about pursuing in their lives. They stroll through their days unengaged and with a lack of energy because they are living a life that has no meaning to them. Legendary football coach Lou Holtz had this to say for individuals who are uninterested in their lives, "If you are bored with life, if you don't get up every morning with a burning desire to do things, you don't have enough goals." If you are not passionate about your life, the first step you need to take is committing to set goals that will inspire you to live better every single day. When you have outcomes that challenge you in unique ways, you will put yourself in the small minority of people that wake up each morning with a burning desire to do unique things.

If you don't get up every morning with a burning desire
to do things, you don't have enough goals.
-@ESPNDrLou

CHARACTERISTICS OF A GOOD GOAL

So, you are now excited about setting goals. You believe in their ability to transform your life and are ready to take the next step. This is the point where most people stall out because they are not exactly sure how to set a goal and how to implement it effectively in their life. This uncertainty usually leads to a lack of follow through because people don't know the first step in how to make their aspirations happen. If this describes you in the past, simply make the decision to follow through and learn what it takes to pursue your best life. However, we are going to lay this process out so that you have everything you need to take initial steps to implement a goal-setting program. We will kick things off with an "I-SMART" criteria that you can use to make sure that you are setting world-class goals that will allow you to maximize performance. Once you can check off yes for each of these criteria, you will be ready to move forward with the implementation phase of goal setting.

CRITERIA #1 - THE "I" FACTOR: It is essential that you believe that you are capable of achieving your goals or your mind will likely find a way to subconsciously sabotage your efforts. To ensure that you are confident in your abilities to make your goals a reality, write your goals in present tense with each starting with the "I" factor. Place the "I" right at the front of your goals and own your ability to achieve them. Eventually, as you write them down each day in this format (e.g., I earn $200,000 in annual income), you will believe in your ability to achieve them and your subconscious brain will get to work on making them happen. It is important to acknowledge that repetition writing your goals in this format is a key to success when pursuing your goals.

CRITERIA #2 - SPECIFIC: This specific checkpoint is one of the most critical elements of goal setting. When it comes to outlining your goals, it is absolutely critical that you are crystal clear about exactly what you would like to achieve. If you are unclear at all in your approach, you will be far more likely to wander in your efforts and the vagueness will allow you to justify lesser efforts when things are challenging. Specificity gives you a clear outcome that defines whether or not you are successful in your efforts, and this ensures that there is no room for justifying anything other than taking proactive steps to make your goals a reality. Once you know what you want (e.g., new job), the key is to narrow in on exactly what job you would want so that you can clearly identify what you need to do to make it happen.

One of the keys to specificity often lies in the ability to measure your goals. If this is not something you can do, then it makes it difficult for you to assess your progress or whether or not you have been successful with your efforts. On top of this, a goal that is not measurable often makes it easier for you to justify underperformance because there is no set standard to gauge the effectiveness of your actions. On the flip side, when a goal has been designed that is measurable, you have the opportunity to know exactly what you need to achieve to be successful. For example, building on the previous job example, if your goal is to get a new job in a specific field at a competitive salary, it makes sense to iron out exactly what a competitive salary means to you so you are able to measure whether you are able to achieve it. This also helps with making sure your subconscious mind knows exactly what to pursue during the job search process. Get specificity right and you will give yourself a legitimate shot at achieving great things moving forward.

CRITERIA #3 - MATTERS: The single most important factor when choosing a goal is deciding on something that truly matters to you. There is nothing that will ensure failure more than choosing something that you are not excited about. Unfortunately, the mistake that most people make is either choosing goals to please others or choosing them to fit within our society. This influence is often challenging to overcome, but it is one that you must because you will not pursue something with your full attention that you are not passionate about. The basic essence of goals is that they are challenging when set properly and you will not fight for them if they are not connected to something that energizes and excites you. So as you write down your goals, make it an absolute priority to be able to check off this criteria before you move on to the other considerations.

> **"There is nothing that will ensure failure more than choosing something that you are not excited about."**
> -@coytecooper

CRITERIA #4 - APPLICABLE: One common mistake that people make when setting goals is that they pursue outcomes without thinking exactly what they hope to achieve in the distant future. In simple terms, they choose goals that have very little to do with their vision and purpose in life. As you can imagine, this often leads to frustration because they are pursuing outcomes that do not allow them to live with purpose. If you want to avoid this frustration, then always ask yourself whether your goal is applicable to what you hope to achieve in the long-term future. For efficiency purposes, it is essential that you set goals that will serve as destination checkpoints for your overall vision. In addition to making you far more effective, it will also allow you to invest in initiatives that will leave you feeling energized and fulfilled.

CRITERIA #5 - REASONABLE: There are two things to consider when visiting the reasonable criteria. First, it is important that you choose goals that are possible given your current circumstances. While it is so critical that you learn to dream big and pursue lofty ambitions, there are also standards that you can set that are so high that they will inevitably lead to failure. For example, if you are a college student, it is not reasonable to set a goal of being the CEO of Apple, GM of the Seattle Seahawks, or United States President in the next year. Setting these types of goals would lead to frustration with the goal setting process. However, there is a fine line on this reasonable criteria because it is important to set goals that would be considered unreasonable by most people's standards. Because the human mind is so spectacular, it can be difficult to sometimes determine exactly what is possible to achieve.

Here is the key. Ask yourself whether or not you think it would be possible to make this aspiration a reality if you did everything within your power to bring it to fruition. If you are still stuck here, ask yourself whether it would be possible for anyone in a similar stage of life to achieve the goal. If the answer is yes to both of these questions, then it is worth pursuing if you are willing to put in the time and energy necessary to make it happen. While you want goals that are possible, it is also important that you have outcomes on your list that are considered "unreasonable" by normal standards. Keep in mind that your ability to dream big will determine where you are able to travel in life. In *The 10X Rule*, best selling author and entrepreneur Grant Cardone explains, "If you approach an endeavor with an average thinking, you will start to give up the moment you come up against any challenges, resistance, or less than optimal conditions - unless you have some big juicy purpose as your engine. To get through resistance, you must have a big reason to get there. The bigger and more unrealistic your goals are - and the more they're aligned with your purpose and duty - the more they'll energize and fuel your actions." When you believe that you have passed both prongs of the reasonable criteria, you are ready to take your final step in the goal development process.

> "To get through resistance, you must have a
> big reason to get there."
> -@GrantCardone

CRITERIA #6 - TIME: The last thing you need to ask yourself when setting goals is whether they are time bound or not. For each of your goals, there should be a deadline in place that creates urgency in your approach. When there is no deadline, it allows you to sit in one place considering what you would need to do to make it a reality. The problem is that goals without a set timeline allow you to continue to sit because you have all the time in the world to achieve them. The moment you put a tangible deadline in place, it forces you to quickly consider the essential steps to success before taking immediate action. One of the simplest ways to achieve this is by starting with one-year goals that will all take place in the next 12-months. If you have chosen goals that meet all of the previous criteria, then you will need to be disciplined every day, week, and month to make them a reality. It is certainly all right for you to set sub-deadlines within the one-year time frame if you believe it is relevant to what you are looking to achieve. However, some of this can also be ironed out in the goal activation steps identified later in the chapter. First, we will visit the concept of goal activation and how to utilize your brain's full potential to make your aspirations a reality.

> ### "The victory of success is half won when one gains the habit of setting and achieving goals."
> ### - Og Mandino

GOAL ACTIVATION

It is important to note that you differentiate yourself the moment you set goals in your life. As explained by former best selling author Og Mandino, "The victory of success is half won when one gains the habit of setting and achieving goals." Even if it is simply setting goals one time (and not writing them down), the act of thinking about them drastically increases your chances of success. In fact, the previous Harvard 10-year study we mentioned in chapter #2 on vision showed that the 13 percent of individuals who simply set goals (and did not revisit them) earned twice as much as individuals who did not write down their goals. This finding alone shows the unique power of your subconscious mind in pursuing outcomes and realizing success. If you were previously not convinced in the goal setting process, hopefully this statistic will put you over the top and inspire you to set them immediately. Once you have done this, the next step is to put yourself in the 3 percent of individuals who outperform the remaining 97 percent by writing down your goals and revisiting them on a daily basis. To succeed in this process, commit to the following five steps to help fully activate your goals.

1. **GET A GOAL BOOK AND MAKE DAILY INVESTMENTS.** If you want to maximize the chances that you realize your goals, you need to make a habit of seeing them every single day. One of the best ways to do this is by getting a goal book and writing down your top three to five one-year goals every single day. As you start this process, make it a

priority to be able to write all of them down from memory as soon as possible. This will ensure that you are programming these goals into your subconscious mind and increasing your chances of success. The best time to engage in this process is during the morning growth routine because it will keep you focused on the initiatives that are most important to you as you start your day. In addition to keeping your mind proactive, it will also allow you to become far more efficient in your decision making because it will make your priorities more clear as you move through your day.

2. PUT THEM IN A PLACE WHERE YOU CAN SEE THEM. The morning is not the only time when you should revisit your goals. In fact, you should see every instance that you revisit them as a repetition that brings you one step closer to reaching your full potential. It is important to point out that we are not talking about looking at them all day long because this would not allow you to get to work making your goals a reality. However, it makes sense to build in at least one opportunity to see your goals during the day to keep you focused and on task. The easiest way to ensure that this occurs is to put your goals in a place where they are visible on a regular basis. This can be on a sheet of paper posted in your office or on your computer desktop that you use throughout your day. This is entirely your call. The key is to put them in locations that are conducive to revisiting them so you hold yourself accountable when there are distractions around demanding your attention.

3. REVISIT THEM RIGHT BEFORE BEDTIME. Once you have written your goals down in the morning and revisited them during the day, there is one more step you can take to drastically increase the chances of making them a reality. As you finish your day, it is important that you revisit your goals one last time before you go to bed. In addition to getting another quality repetition, this activity allows you to bring your goals to your subconscious mind's attention so it can get to work on figuring out how to achieve them while you sleep. It is a simple step with high impact potential, but you must have the self-discipline to follow through if you are going to realize the benefits associated with this activity.

4. SHARE THEM WITH A FRIEND. Research has shown that you can increase your chances of realizing your goals by 25 percent by simply sharing them with a friend. If you are wondering why this would be the case, it is because telling someone makes the goal more real and adds an accountability measure. After all, if you tell someone, they are aware of your aspirations and they will know if you decide to give up on them. This alone is often enough to motivate you because you will not want someone thinking that you quit. However, the more important aspect is that sharing the goal will help solidify the fact that the goal is meaningful and that you plan to make it a reality in your life. So, get your goals in place and go out and share them as soon as possible so you can start the pursuit to live your best life.

> " Research has shown you can increase your chances of achieving goals by 25% by sharing them with a friend.
> -@coytecooper "

5. PRACTICE IMMEDIATE ACTION IMPLEMENTATION. The final step in implementing your goals is to take immediate action. Not tomorrow. Not next week. NOW. Do something immediately to move towards your goal. It doesn't have to be something major, but it does have to be something tangible that will allow you to build momentum. You can get this process in motion by brainstorming exactly what it will take to make your goals a reality. Once you come upon action items that are essential to the realization of your aspirations, write them down and make it a top priority to work them into your daily schedule. These small steps will immediately start to build momentum and will become a part of your plan to achieve your goals. In the words of legendary artist Pablo Picasso, "Our goals can only be reached through a vehicle of a plan, in which we must fervently believe, and upon which we must vigorously act. There is no other route to success." You do not need to have all the answers, but you do need to take action so that you can move towards your goals. This needs to be a habit every single day if you are going to reach your full potential.

Pursue Goals, But Keep Perspective

Pursue your goals with your full attention every single day. Make it a top priority to bring them to fruition in your life. However, do not get so obsessed with the end outcome that you lose track of the fact that your pursuit is a part of a larger journey. The reality is that you will not be successful in the realization of every single goal that you set, every time that you set them. There will be times where you fall short of expectations. In these moments, keep in mind this quote by best selling author Les Brown: "You may not accomplish every goal you set - no one does - but what really matters is having goals and going after them wholeheartedly. In the end, it is the person you become, not the things you achieve, that is most important." The pursuit of goals will transform you into a completely different person if you fully invest in the process. This will be an ongoing journey and eventually you will get the chance to achieve things that you previously never thought possible. But first you must choose aims that unleash the power of the goal setting process. To do this, take this advice from the legendary entrepreneur Andrew Carnegie: "If you want to be happy, set a goal that commands your thoughts, liberates your energy, and inspires your hope." Once you have these types of goals in place, the remaining process is simple. Be willing to do the little things consistently each day that most people are simply not willing to do.   Earn the right to live your goals. Start making investments today.

THE MAKE YOUR MARK MARK MASTER

KYLE DAKE

In the sport of wrestling, there are few people who have achieved more than Kyle Dake in college wrestling. In terms of unique accomplishments, he was able to do something that no one in the history of the sport has ever been able to do. In four years as a Varsity starter at Cornell University, Dake compiled a record of 132-4 and won 4 straight NCAA Wrestling Championships, all at four different weight classes. While he was absolutely a gifted athlete, the thing that truly made him unique was his mental approach to competition. From the moment he stepped on Cornell's campus, Dake had it in his mind that he was going to win an NCAA Championship as a true freshman. To make sure that his mind truly believed this, he wrote down his goal of winning an NCAA Championship every single day and consistently visualized himself on top of the podium. When it came time to compete during primetime on ESPN, he was ready to capitalize on the opportunity. The end result of this masterful goal setting process was a historic run that may never be matched in the sport.

KEY SUMMARY POINTS

○ Goals serve as checkpoints for your dreams and allow you to progress efficiently and purposefully on a day-to-day basis.

○ Only 8 percent of people follow through on their intentions. Learning how to implement goals will drastically increase your chances of success while filling your days with energy.

○ Good goals have specific criteria that will help you to identify specific aims to pursue on a daily basis. Getting these criteria correct will make you far more efficient in your efforts in the long run.

○ Intentionally activating your goals is an essential element for engaging your subconscious brain so you can progress towards your aspirations every minute of the day.

'S INEVITABLE. PURSUE THE THING YOU ARE MEANT TO DO ALL OUT AND MAKING YOUR MARK IS INEVITABLE. PURS

Chapter 6

Develop the Discipline Required to Live Your Dreams

> Have you built your castles in the air? Good. That is where they should be built. Now, go to work and build foundations under them.
> - Henry David Thoreau

Goals are meant to be lofty. In fact, when set properly, they should take you way out of your comfort zone and require you to grow tremendously if you want to bring them to fruition. This is a major part of what goals are all about and this is what makes them so impactful. While they are absolutely meant to help you achieve specific ambitions, the ability to pursue target outcomes also allows you to grow and evolve into a completely different person. However, in the words of Henry David Thoreau, you must first learn to build your castles in the air because "this is where they should be built." Then you go out and get to work building a solid foundation that includes self-discipline and a world-class ability to follow through on your intentions. You simply must learn to embrace the fundamentals if you want to make your aspirations a reality. This chapter is all about helping you cultivate this discipline so you have the approach and skill sets necessary to realize all of your dreams.

IMPLEMENTING YOUR INTENTIONS

One of the most common reasons why people do not realize their dreams is that they have no idea what they would like to achieve in life. This makes sense, right? Your chances of bumping in to your dreams are slim to none if you have no idea what it is that you want to achieve. This concept is the same for goals. However, there is another culprit that just as commonly robs people of their ability to achieve their aspirations. The number of people who have occasional dreams that flash through their minds about the type of life they would like to live are a dime a dozen. The problem is that they do not want these things bad enough to get out of their comfort zone and follow through on their intentions. They have failed to grasp the concept that when you find a desirable vision that is in alignment with your purpose, you must decide whether you are willing to fight for it.

When it matters enough, you will rearrange your life so you are able to dedicate the time and energy necessary to make your goal a reality. In today's society, the problem is that most people do not have the desire and/or self-discipline necessary to go out and earn the right to live their dreams. Because of this, they lack the grit to make the smaller investments that are necessary to progress and realize lofty aspirations. While this is often the result of laziness, another cause is the unrealistic expectations that have been created with our instant gratification culture.

 Most people do not have the desire or self-discipline necessary to earn the right to live their dreams.

-@coytecooper

Instant Gratification and Unrealistic Expectations

We live in a society that has cultivated unrealistic expectations where people believe they automatically deserve success and they expect it to come quickly. The issue with this mentality is that it is counterintuitive to how meaningful accomplishments come to fruition. Unfortunately, the American culture has become obsessed with instant gratification and success. One primary example is the fast food industry in the United States. It has been founded around the premise of instant gratification and thrives on providing people with immediate pleasure at a low price point. Studies have shown that millions of people in the United States set health goals each year, but only 27 percent of these individuals follow through and make them a reality. One of the primary reasons why so many people fail in this area is because of the challenge that comes with dietary adjustments. While many people aspire to improve their health at some point in their life, most give in to the desire for instant gratification, as it is the easy route to feeling good immediately. Unfortunately for them, this is a short-term approach and people end up frustrated and unfulfilled because taking the easy route will not bring meaning to their lives. Deep down we all know that this is not the right way to live and we long for a life where we strive for something much more.

Another example of this immediate expectation mentality is the entertainment industry, where individuals have regularly been elevated to a "superstar" status who lack values and have done very little to actually earn the success they are experiencing. One common example is the individuals who have emerged into "stardom" from reality shows that our younger generations are watching on a regular basis. Because these individuals are put on television, featured on magazine covers, and are trending on social media, they are seen as role models and younger generations strive to be just like them. The problem with this situation is that it creates a distorted view of meaningful success and exactly what it takes to achieve it. In the words of bestselling author of *The Compound Effect* and elite entrepreneur Darren Hardy, "As a society, we have been deceived. We've been hypnotized by commercial marketing, which convinces you of problems you don't have and sells you on the idea of insta-fixes to 'cure' them. We've been socialized to believe in the fairy-tale endings found in movies and novels. We've lost sight of the good, old-fashioned value of hard and consistent work." The reality is that the best accomplishments are ones that you have to work hard to achieve over an extended period of time. This is what makes them so special. You must earn them through discipline, sacrifice, and hard work that allows you to reach full potential as a person. If you want to live a life that is full of meaning and worthy of your full attention, you need to choose the right destination and then you need to earn the right to go there in the future.

 Cemeteries are full of unfulfilled dreams...Don't choose to walk the well-worn path to regret.

-@SteveMaraboli

The Secret to Success

If you are expecting some groundbreaking secret that makes success easy, then you may be disappointed with this section. We have already uncovered one of the key elements to success earlier in this book when outlining vision. All high performers in life have a unique vision that they are passionate about and they have the creativity and self-discipline to make plans to go there. This is a foundational element that you must master if you want to live an extraordinary life where you make your mark on the world. However, as we have already mentioned, this step alone will guarantee nothing. There are all kinds of people in this world who have an aspiration they would like to achieve, but they have never done anything to make it a reality. Bestselling author Dr. Steve Maraboli explained this about failing to follow through on your intentions: "Cemeteries are full of unfulfilled dreams...countless echoes of 'could have' and 'should have'...Don't choose to walk the well-worn path to regret." If you want to avoid this path of mediocrity, then you must learn to take action immediately to realize your goals and live your dreams. If you don't believe me, then listen to this potentially life altering advice by talk show host, entrepreneur, and philanthropist Oprah Winfrey: "The big secret in life is that there is no secret. Whatever is your goal, you can get there if you are willing to work." When it comes to extraordinary accomplishments, there is simply no other route to achievement than developing world-class self-discipline that guides you in making consistent daily investments to earn the right to live your dreams.

THE ROLE OF DISCIPLINE IN LIVING YOUR DREAMS

The basic premise of lofty aspirations is that they are out of your reach and you must stretch in order to achieve them. Because you do not have the capacity to achieve them at the moment, it is imperative that you learn to make investments so you are able to progress towards your end destination. This is where your self-discipline comes in to play. As explained by legendary author and motivational speaker Jim Rohn, "Discipline is the bridge between goals and accomplishment." Continuing with this theme, see your goal as a destination across a large body of water where there is no easy, visible way to reach the other side. If the end destination is important enough to you (and the end location is a much better situation than your current one), then you will immediately search to find a way to get across the body of water. Given that you have already chosen extraordinary goals in the previous chapter, we will assume that you are ready to find a way to cross the body of water to reach your end destination. Because there is no short cut available, you are left with no other choice than to create a reliable route to realize your goal. You must build the bridge or vessel to cross the body of water in the most efficient manner. The only way to make this happen is if you are willing to make daily investments over time to earn the right to reach your end destination.

 Discipline is the bridge between goals and accomplishment.
- Jim Rohn

DAILY DOSES OF DISCIPLINE

One of the most challenging aspects of lofty goals is the fact that you must invest over time to earn the right to achieve them. It is an extremely difficult concept for many to embrace because you need to learn to be able to follow through when an end outcome is not in sight. This is the exact time when highly successful people learn to get to work. They are not deterred by the fact that their goals and dreams are in the distant future because they have embraced the concept of "daily doses of discipline" and doing the little things each day to progress steadily towards their dreams. Former United States President Theodore Roosevelt had this to say about self-discipline: "The one quality which sets one person apart from another - the key which lifts one to every aspiration while others are caught up in the mire of mediocrity - is not talent, formal education, nor intellectual brightness - it is self-discipline. With self-discipline, all things are possible. Without it, even the simplest goal can seem like an impossible dream." No doubt that President Roosevelt understood that success is more like a journey where you must make small, seemingly insignificant investments to reach your end destination. There is simply no room for taking shortcuts in this approach. It is all about cultivating world-class self-discipline and learning to make daily impactful intentions.

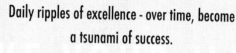

> Daily ripples of excellence - over time, become
> a tsunami of success.
> -@_robin_sharma

INSTANT GRATIFICATION VS. IMPACTFUL INVESTMENTS

One of the most profound concepts when it comes to success is the realization that it is within reach for anyone who is willing to sacrifice and make impactful investments on a daily basis over an extended period of time. This has often been referred to as the one percent improvement approach. While alone these one percent investments are not profound, over time they compound and they turn into something truly extraordinary. In the words of Robin Sharma, "Daily ripples of excellence - over time, become a tsunami of success." It is important to point this out because it means that success is not something that is out of reach and determined by uncontrollable circumstances. Instead, it is a choice that you make every single day when you make decisions. In moments where you are contemplating following through on your intentions, you are often presented with the choice between instant gratification and sacrificing to make impactful investments. For example, with the structure provided in this book, you now have the opportunity to invest in a morning growth routine that can and will transform your life if you commit to it. The decision to invest in this routine is your intention. While this intention is a great starting point, there will come a moment where you will have a decision to make because your bed will be comfortable and you will not be ready to get out from under your warm blankets. This little voice in your head encouraging you to sleep a little longer represents the instant gratification route. At this moment, we either choose this route or we decide to get up and follow through on our intentions (with our vision in mind). This is referred to as the impactful investment route. The instant gratification route is enjoyable in the immediate short-term, but will lead to frustration in the long-term because you have chosen not to follow through on your intentions. The impactful investment route will be challenging in the short-term, but extremely rewarding in the long-term because you will be making a decision to pursue your best life. We have basic decisions like this throughout each of our days. In the moments where you are considering not following through on your intentions, do not underestimate the value of individual decisions. Given the value of single investments, what you are really choosing between is a mediocre life or an extraordinary one so choose wisely.

 The importance of repetition until automaticity cannot be overstated. Repetition is the key to learning.
- John Wooden

GETTING YOUR REPS IN

In the world of competitive athletics, one of the ways that you break down your progress during preparation is by getting repetitions in during practice. This process, often referred to as reps, has become a critical way to measure whether you are preparing well enough to excel during competition. Regardless of your sport (whether individual or team), it is all about getting your reps in so you can hone your skills and perform at a high competitive level. It becomes a tangible way to help people progress towards their goals more efficiently because you are able to dictate the reps necessary each day to improve. Legendary UCLA Basketball coach John Wooden explained that "The importance of repetition until automaticity cannot be overstated. Repetition is the key to learning." Interestingly, this is not a concept that has become commonplace in normal, non-athletic environments. However, it certainly should be because it is very much applicable to achieving success in every area of life. In the area of your personal growth, it is an essential component because it allows you to break down your daily activities and progression into individual steps. In addition to providing clarity in your overall approach, the process provides you with tangible daily steps that are far less overwhelming because they focus on individual investments rather than attempting to accomplish the entire goal at one time.

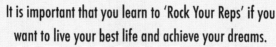

> It is important that you learn to 'Rock Your Reps' if you want to live your best life and achieve your dreams.
> -@coytecooper

From a personal standpoint, your repetitions should become all of the key initiatives outlined in this book that are designed to maximize your personal growth so you can move towards your full potential. Each time that you follow through on revisiting your dreams and goals, it is a rep that allows you to strengthen your ability to achieve them. It also happens to reinforce the message of exactly what you would like to accomplish to your subconscious mind. When you follow through on your action item steps that are necessary to realize your goals, you are putting in a repetition that builds self-discipline that is essential for achieving unique things. As you read for 30-minutes each morning, you get a rep towards cultivating skill sets that are necessary to perform at your highest level. All of these are investments you can make each day that will compound and help you to earn the right to live your dreams. It is important that you learn to "rock your reps" if you want to live your best life and make this happen.

How to "Rock Your Reps" in Everyday Living

One of my favorite quotes that I have made a habit of revisiting on a daily basis is by bestselling author and motivator Robin Sharma. He explains that "success is the masterful application of the fundamentals on a daily basis" and that it is all about "stringing a series of well lived days together like a string of pearls." The key here is getting exceptional at embracing interactions on a daily basis so you eventually get the opportunity to string together masterful days and weeks. Eventually, this process allows you to live outstanding months and years that drastically transform your life. The first step to achieving this type of life is identifying the exact reps that you will rock on your way to realizing your goals and living your dreams. These will become your daily action item plan that will guide your decisions on a regular basis. Once you know what is included in this plan, it is all about developing the self-discipline to follow through on these intentions. As you develop the ability to "rock your reps" on a daily basis, you will eventually start to string together masterful days that will eventually turn into masterful weeks, months, and years. With consistent investments, your life will turn into something truly extraordinary because you will have learned to embrace the "little things" that most people neglect. While following through and establishing discipline are challenging steps, they are always worth the investment because they provide you with a foundational skill to live a remarkable life. The key thing now is to identify the exact reps you will rock each day to realize your dreams and live your best life.

Success is all about stringing a series of well lived days together like a string of pearls.

-@_robin_sharma

Five Steps to Rock Your Reps

As you progress in your personal growth journey, it will be important that you identify the exact reps that you are passionate about embracing on a regular basis. It is essential that you choose meaningful activities that will allow you to progress towards your aspirations. Given that people are so different from each other, this means that there will inevitably be variations in the activities that people choose to implement in their daily rep routine. This is something that should be embraced from one person to the next. With that being said, there are core elements that should always be a part of your pursuit to realize your dreams and goals. When success leaves traces, it is your job to find them so you can embrace principles that are conducive to high performance levels. This is exactly why the "Five Steps to Rock Your Reps" were created. These are five powerful initiatives that you can embrace to put yourself on the path to success. You will recognize some of these as we have covered them at some point earlier in the book. Others will be completely new and you will need to work harder to make them a part of your daily routine. Become a master at rocking these reps and your life will never be the same!

STEP #1: EMBRACE THE MORNING ROUTINE. We have already touched on how important it is to invest in a morning growth routine that sets the tone for your entire day. However, there is another reason why you need to invest in this early morning ritual. When it comes to goals, it is absolutely essential that you fully believe that you deserve the right to live them. There can be no doubts if you want to make them a reality. If you want to cultivate the confidence necessary to realize your aspirations, you need to take advantage of the early morning to direct your focus sharply in the direction of your dreams. Make it a habit to write your goals down every single morning and surround them with reading materials and journal entries that reinforce their achievement. The same can be said for your dreams. This is the exact type of structure that will keep you focused on progression in high priority areas when life is crazy all around you. It is absolutely essential that you learn to block out the clutter and the morning routine will help make this happen if you have the discipline to do it every single day.

STEP #2: IMPLEMENT IMMEDIATE ACTION ITEMS. It is not enough to simply revisit your goals on a daily basis. As we touched upon in the previous section, your success will depend on your ability to identify and move on meaningful action item steps in your daily schedule. The first step to making this happen is prioritizing your goals so you can initially narrow in on your top three based on their level of importance. These are the goals that will energize you when you think about them. It is smart to narrow on select goals as you get started because it will help you from getting overwhelmed as you master the process. Once you have clarity on your top three goals, the next progression is to sit down and brainstorm action items steps that you can take on a consistent basis to bring your one-year goals to fruition. Goal expert and best selling author Brian Tracy refers to this strategic planning process as "mindstorming" and suggests that you write down as many strategies as you can possibly think of that will allow you to progress towards your goals. As you get started, identify five to 10 things that you can follow through on within the next year and two to three that you can implement immediately in the next week. Be sure to do this activity for your top three goals in a three-week span and start taking action to move towards your top goal immediately. These steps will allow you to build momentum that will put you on the path to success. Once you have a good grasp on your top three goals, you can start to invest in this process for your other goals so you take intentional steps to make them a reality as well.

STEP #3: MASTER THE ART OF AUTOSUGGESTION. In *Think and Grow*

Rich, Napoleon Hill explains that autosuggestion is the process of focusing on the thing you want with intensity until it becomes a healthy desire. In essence, autosuggestion is the process of getting in the habit of suggesting the things that you would like to achieve to your subconscious mind. In simple terms, this involves the habit of intentionally sending specific messages to your brain on a regular basis to cultivate a proactive mindset. Best selling author Anthony Robbins alludes to this process when touching on affirmations and the importance of repeating positive statements to yourself that relate to your vision. If you know that confidence will be essential to achieve your dreams, then he would likely suggest that you repeat a statement like the following with intensity each day until you master the approach you desire: "I am a highly confident person who fully believes in my ability to achieve extraordinary things." While this sounds a little crazy and you may be uncomfortable as you start this process, the constant investment in this process will eventually make it feel normal and your subconscious mind will eventually embrace the statement as if it were true. The ability to rock reps in this area will allow you to train your mind to think exactly the way you would like it to in the future.

> "Autosuggestion is the process of focusing on what you want with intensity until it becomes a healthy desire.
>
> -@coytecooper

STEP #4: PRACTICE DAILY VISUALIZATION. There is little doubt that lofty goals are going to require an adjustment in your mental approach to achieve them. In fact, if you have set your aspirations high enough, you will need to stretch your mind beyond its current capacity so you are able to pursue them with full confidence. Why is this so important? Well, if you don't have confidence, it is inevitable that you will hold back in your efforts because you will likely not believe that your goals are possible. The good news is that the first three steps are designed to build confidence and train your mind to believe in your ability to achieve unique things. Building on these steps, it would be highly beneficial to get in the habit of visualizing yourself achieving your dreams and goals on a regular basis. Similar to vision, they may be cloudy at first, but this will eventually move towards being crystal clear as you get your daily reps in. Once you revisit your goals in the morning, pick your top one and go to a place that is quiet where you can concentrate well. Close your eyes and visualize what this accomplishment will look and feel like when you realize it. If it has to do with other people, picture yourself impacting them and seeing their lives change as a result. If it has to do with an athletic accomplishment, visualize yourself in the actual stadium hitting the winning shot and the crowd going wild. Get in the habit of seeing yourself making the goal a reality so your mind has no choice but to believe that it will come true.

STEP #5: ALLOW YOUR GOALS TO EVOLVE. When you invest in the steps outlined in this book, it is absolutely inevitable that you will grow and move towards your full potential. In fact, it will likely happen at a rate so rapid that the drastic change in your mindset will astonish you. With this being the case, it is natural that you will need to allow your goals to evolve at a similar pace. It should not alarm you if you outgrow your goals and need to adjust your aspirations to challenge you in a meaningful way. If you realize that one or more of your goals are no longer important to you, then simply take it off of your list and replace it with something more in alignment with your skill sets and vision. If your lower tier goals start to have a higher level of importance to you, do not hesitate to move them up the list and revisit the action item progression so you can make it a priority in your daily schedule. The point is that you should expect to outgrow your goals at some point when you are investing in the right reps. As you progress, continue to elevate your goals so you rise to a level that is closer to your vision.

GETTING YOUR MIND'S FULL ATTENTION

In *The Compound Effect*, author Darren Hardy explains that, "we are bombarded with billions of sensory (visual, audio, physical) bites of information each day. To keep ourselves from going insane, we ignore 99.9 percent of them, only really seeing, hearing, or experiencing those upon which our mind focuses." When you learn to rock your reps on a consistent basis and focus sharply on your vision, you are reiterating the importance of your goals to your brain and it is inevitable that it will eventually see them as a top priority. When this happens, it will move into the .1 percent of the sensory that your mind is constantly aware of and you will consistently notice opportunities to progress towards your dreams. This will allow you to use your full mental capacity to pursue your goals on a daily basis. This drastically increases your chances of achieving your aspirations, and because they are in alignment with your vision, you will constantly progress towards living your dreams and best life. To make sure this occurs, it is important that you have chosen goals that truly stretch you and take you way out of your comfort zone.

> **If your dreams do not scare you, they are not big enough.**
> - Ellen Johnson Sirleaf

IF THEY DON'T SCARE YOU...

In a speech to Harvard graduates, Ellen Johnson Sirleaf, the 24th President of Liberia, explained that, "if your dreams do not scare you, then they are not big enough." As humans, we have amazing potential that is rarely realized because most of us place significant limitations on what is realistic to achieve. The reality is that you have no idea of what is really possible if you are not willing to dream big and pursue your passions. While goals are shorter-term in nature, the same concept holds true if you want to realize your full potential. As you sit down to iron out your dreams and goals, be sure that you have chosen some that make you uncomfortable. It is completely normal if you choose dreams that inspire you, but you have no idea at the moment how you will achieve them. This part will scare you, but it is really important that you do not allow this to scare you off. The real danger lies in choosing goals and dreams that are comfortable because they will not challenge you to move towards full potential. As explained by best selling author Grant Cardone, "The reality is that if you start small, you are probably going to go small. People's failure to think big enough usually means they will never act big enough, often enough, or persistently enough. After all, who gets excited about so-called realistic goals?" The lesson here is to go big and choose aspirations that scare you. Stand your ground and invest heavily in the process outlined in this book so you can make them a reality. Set extremely high standards in your approach and be willing to invest in the right initiatives each day so you can compound your efforts over time. Eventually, you will start to grow into your dreams and they will no longer scare you. This is when you will know it is time to achieve them so you can move on to new ones that scare you again.

> The reality is that if you start small, you are probably going to go small.
> -@GrantCardone

Seeing The Bigger Picture

Goals are absolutely going to be about you pursuing excellence in key areas of life that matter to you. The process in this chapter is designed to stretch you so that you are able to progress towards your dreams. However, as we have mentioned once before, the investment in goals is also about you transforming yourself as a person. In the words of the legendary motivator Zig Ziglar, "What you get by achieving your goals is not as important as what you become by achieving your goals." While you will be focused on your outcomes, an interesting thing will happen when you get in the habit of investing in yourself and living each day masterfully while pursuing your goals. Eventually, you will evolve into a completely different person who has much different aspirations than when you started your journey. It is likely that the investment and internal reflection brings you to a place where you are inspired by the opportunity to change people's lives and to make your mark on the world. This is when your goals will shift to include things that improve the quality of life for others. Microsoft founder, billionaire, and philanthropist Bill Gates refers to this as "improving the human condition" and explains that goals are critical to this process. When this time comes, the good news is that you will know how to set goals worthy of your attention and with the potential to impact the world.

> **What you get by achieving your goals is not as important as what you become by achieving your goals.**
> -Zig Ziglar

MICHAEL JORDAN

Michael Jordan is one of the greatest basketball players to ever play the game, and likely one of the best athletes the world has ever known. However, this was not always the case for Michael. In his book *I Can't Accept Not Trying*, he explains that he was cut from the varsity basketball team as a sophomore and had a decision to make about his future. After pondering his level of commitment, he decided that he never wanted to feel that way again and immediately set a goal to be a varsity starter the next year. He got to work during the summer every single day working on tangible areas that would improve his game and allow him to realize his goal. As he progressed, he set new goals so that he would know exactly where he wanted to go and then he would pursue them with his full attention. These efforts compounded and he realized his goal the next year. In addition, his commitment to setting and pursuing goals continued to impact his approach as he went on to become an All-American in college at the University of North Carolina and eventually a six-time NBA champion and five-time Most Valuable Player (MVP) in the National Basketball Association (NBA).

KEY SUMMARY POINTS

O   Instant gratification and unrealistic expectations are two things that plague our society and are the primary reasons so many people fail to live their best lives. You must shun both of these philosophies if you want to achieve remarkable accomplishments that make an impact on the world.

O   One of the essential elements to meaningful success is embracing a mindset where you expect to earn the right to live your goals and dreams. Take pride in knowing that you are making investments that will allow you to realize your full potential as a human being.

O   Getting the right reps in each day will build your confidence and equip you with the necessary skill sets to achieve your aspirations in the future. These must be performed on a daily basis if you want to progress towards your aspirations.

O   Your dreams, when set properly, should scare you a little and will require that you get out of your comfort zone to make them a reality. If you are living in your comfort zone on a regular basis, then you have likely set goals that are not worthy of your full attention.

Chapter 7

Clear the Clutter and Focus on What Truly Matters

"
Simplicity is the ultimate sophistication.
- Leonardo Di Vinci
"

One of the greatest challenges in life is learning to "clear the clutter" so you can focus all of your time and energy on the things that matter most to you. The fascinating part of life is that we are often tricked into believing that being busier with more things is the key to success. It is the "more is better" philosophy that robs so many people of their dreams. Here is the exact reason why. We consistently take on more obligations with little regard to whether they align with our vision or not. In pursuit of pleasing everyone else, we say yes far too many times to average opportunities and eventually fill our plates with things that have nothing to do with our dreams and goals. And while this may allow us to progress in our careers, it leaves us with a feeling of emptiness and being unfulfilled because we are not spending our time on things that truly matter to us. In short, we are not pursuing our purpose and as a result we have little to no passion in our lives. If you want to live a life full of meaning, you need to find a way to clear this clutter so you can spend more time on the things that truly matter to you.

NEVER NEGLECT THINGS THAT MATTER MOST

As humans, we have become efficient at being able to tell others the things that we perceive to be most important to us in our life. For many people, when asked this, they will say that it is their family. No matter how much you grow and learn about yourself, this should always be at the top of your list. From a theoretical standpoint, it seems that most people have a basic understanding of some of the things they should be investing in to live their best lives. The problem is that this often becomes lip service for most people. While they can easily tell you that family is most important to them, their actions are not in alignment with this priority area when you take a look at their schedule. When something is truly important to you, it will show in the amount of time and energy you put towards making that area remarkable. So, whether it is family or something else you see as a top value, you need to take a look at how much time and energy you are investing in the area to ensure you are progressing towards your full potential. Never neglect the things that matter most to you or eventually you may not have them in your life.

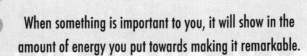

When something is important to you, it will show in the amount of energy you put towards making it remarkable.

-@coytecooper

LIFE IS SIMPLE...WELL, AT LEAST IT SHOULD BE

Life is not designed to be overly complex. In the words of Confucius, "Life is really simple, but we insist on making it complicated."

We often make it this way because we are poor at determining how to spend our time each day. One of the biggest culprits is the habit of saying yes to other people even when we have no interest in the thing they are offering up. While we all must do some things like this in our personal and professional lives, the problem comes when your entire day is made up of performing tasks for others that have no alignment with your vision. If this resonates with you, then you need to learn to say no whenever feasible so you can spend more time on "passion initiatives" that allow you to progress towards your goals and dreams. At the very least, you need to make adjustments so that your time ratio should be in favor of these "passion initiatives" over the "obligation initiatives." It may be difficult to accomplish this in your professional life depending on your responsibilities, but you can certainly make adjustments in your personal time so you are spending more time on initiatives that energize you.

 Life is really simple, but we insist on making it complicated.
-Confucius

THE ULTIMATE SOPHISTICATION

We often try to do far too much with our days. It is as if we have correlated success with being able to finish as many tasks as possible in a single day. As a result, we often end up spending our time spread out among a wide array of menial tasks that keep us preoccupied from early morning until the time we go to bed. Yet at the end of the day, we do not feel as if we have achieved anything significant and go to bed exhausted. Our intentions are good in our approach to achieve success, but our strategy is not effective because we have made things far too complicated. We are also spending most of our time on activities that have little alignment with our goals and dreams. In the words of French poet Antoine de Saint-Exupery, "Perfection is achieved, not when there is nothing more to add, but when there is nothing left to take away." Your job is to heed this advice so that you can experience the ultimate sophistication in life that comes with a simple approach. This involves eliminating daily activities and thoughts that do not contribute to your core aspirations. Once you have cleared the clutter from your life, focus on allowing your vision to dictate how you live in all areas of your life.

ALLOW VISION TO CHOOSE YOUR LIFESTYLE

The key to living an extraordinary life where you achieve remarkable things lies in your ability to allow your vision to choose your lifestyle. The first step to making this happen is investing in personal growth so that you can identify a vision that energizes you and taps into your area(s) of genius. Once you have invested enough time in this process, your vision will become clear and you will start to build momentum. This is when you need to learn how to allow your vision to determine your lifestyle. In simple terms, when you know where you want to go, you will start to understand the daily activities that will and will not allow you to go there. In the words of bestselling author Myles Munroe, "vision should determine your lifestyle" and will ultimately dictate how you live your life each day if your desire to achieve it is strong enough. In these instances, it will influence how you choose your friends, hobbies, entertainment, diet, library, priorities, daily actions, and life plan. He goes on to explain that vision should ultimately drive how you use your time, how you use your energy, and how you invest your money. It is your ability to make the right decisions in these areas that will determine the success you realize in life.

THE LIFESTYLE OF LEGACY

Most people choose a lifestyle based on the path of least resistance. They want to be comfortable so they constantly make decisions that allow them to remain in their safe zone. The issue with this approach is that it will never allow you to reach full potential. You have no chance of accomplishing something extraordinary and making your mark on the world if you make decisions based on what is easiest. Instead, you need to adjust your mindset and cultivate a "lifestyle of legacy" where you are able to live a life that is worth remembering once you have passed. The path to leaving your legacy will begin when you choose a set of dreams that inspire you to live your absolute best life. When you find this desirable path, you will be energized by the opportunity to live the right way because you will have found your meaning for life. This will serve as the initial legacy that you hope to leave and will help dictate your lifestyle. Former NFL coach Tony Dungy explained this about legacy: "It's about the journey--mine and yours--and the lives we can touch, the legacy we can leave, and the world we can change for the better." Choose the right path because it will ensure that you have no regrets at the end of your life. That is, when you have the discipline to make sound decisions consistently each day that help you earn the privilege to live your dreams.

> " It's about the journey–mine and yours...the lives we can touch, and the world we can change for the better. "
> -@tonydungy

So, from a practical standpoint, what exactly does it mean to allow your vision to choose your lifestyle? That's a fair question as theoretical concepts are often difficult to apply to real life situations without tangible examples. Let's start with some specific examples that come from people I have had the opportunity to work with recently in their pursuit to dream big while setting tangible goals and action item steps. Fox Baldwin is an ambitious young man who competes for the University of Virginia as a student-athlete. Because he is a natural dreamer, he has set lofty aspirations that will require him to live a very demanding lifestyle if he is going to make them a reality. One of his primary aims while in college is to become a 4x NCAA Wrestling Champion. To put this into context, this is a feat that has only been accomplished by a handful of wrestlers in the history of the sport. It is an extremely challenging accomplishment that will take a rare blend of talent and a uniquely disciplined lifestyle. While he cannot completely control the natural talent area, he can absolutely maximize his chances of making it a reality by allowing his vision to dictate all of his decisions he makes once he arrives on campus. For anyone who has gone to college, you know that there will be distractions that will immediately threaten his ability to live the lifestyle that is conducive to living his dream. To perform at an elite level, he is going to have to say no regularly to the normal college social life so he is able to focus his full attention towards performing to his peak performance potential (and to succeed in academics which he has lofty goals for as well). On top of this, he will need to choose a diet that maximizes energy and speeds up the recovery process so he can get extra reps in. Every single decision that he makes in a day will impact his ability to pursue his dreams, and he must remember this as distractions around him threaten to steal his focus. His entire daily approach, and all of his decisions, will need to align with his vision so he gives himself the best shot at realizing his goal of becoming a 4x NCAA Champion.

I am blessed to have had the chance to work with another talented young professional named Christina who has a dream of giving a TED talk on a topic that will help drastically change lives in impoverished nations. She is passionate about empowering people in these countries so they can be self-sustainable and thrive in the future. She is another dreamer who has set a lofty vision that will take some serious discipline and hard work to make it a reality. If you are this far in the book, we can assume that you plan to be a dreamer as well. If so, then Christina's situation will help you grasp this concept. Now back to the TED talk. If she is going to achieve this lofty aspiration, then her vision is going to need to dictate her daily decisions. Let's start with her time demands. As a student at the University of North Carolina at Chapel Hill, she is going to have limited time on her hands to pursue her vision, as it is a top public institution with challenging expectations. However, it is absolutely something she can overcome if she is disciplined in her daily approach. It will start with her decisions in the area of entertainment. Rather than spend her weekends socializing, she will need to say no to normal activities so she is able to allocate time to building her knowledge in the TED topic area. It will also be essential for her to be intentional about choosing books, audio recordings, and videos that allow her to become an expert in her area of focus. If she wants the energy to extend her days so she is able to accomplish more, her diet will need to be healthy so she is able to provide her body with the nutrients needed to perform at a high level. It will also be important to choose friends that will support her dreams and encourage her to pursue them. In each of these areas previously mentioned by Dr. Myles Munroe, she is going to be tested on how much she wants to achieve her goal. If her "why" is strong enough, she will make decisions that allow her to progress consistently towards her vision. Nothing is guaranteed, but this will give her the best shot to live her dream.

STRIVE FOR ONE GRAND OF GROWTH

One of the most common mistakes that people make when setting off to pursue a lofty ambition is they believe they have to accomplish it all at one time. Even worse, they may be entitled and expect it to come quickly and easily. Either route will lead you to a disappointing outcome. Another common occurrence is that people often become overwhelmed with the magnitude of their dreams and back off from their pursuit because they question their ability to achieve them. Neither Christina nor Fox can allow this to happen if they are going to have a chance to live their dreams moving forward. Rather than focus on these unproductive thoughts, growth and success guru Brian Tracy recommends that you instead strive to become a 1000% person. This is actually far simpler and less intimidating than it sounds. He explains that your focus should be on consistent improvement and striving to be at least 1/1000th better each and every day. This is something that anyone with the right approach can achieve. While this alone seems like an insignificant amount, he demonstrates that this small improvement compounds over time and ends up being a 26% increase over the course of the year. Does this sound intriguing to you? If so, then read on because the next example will allow you to realize this amount of growth and more in your life. That is, if you are disciplined enough to follow through and capitalize on the compound effect.

Do you remember the morning routine that we discussed earlier in the book? This is an ideal example of core activities that will completely transform your life if you do them consistently over the next year. Still not convinced? Then consider the following data about this set of activities. If you get up early each morning to invest in a morning routine, this will likely include 30 minutes of reading, 10 minutes of journaling, and 5-minutes of revisiting your goals. That would be a fairly basic approach that would take 45-minutes of your time. While alone this seems pretty inconsequential, if you are consistent with your efforts, these investments will eventually add up to a staggering amount of time over the course of the year. It seems hard to believe that a 45-minute investment each day results in the equivalent of nearly seven full 40 hour work weeks of personal growth in this time frame. This is exactly the type of investment that will allow you to become at least 1/1000th better every single day. Still not sold? Maybe the 26% increase just isn't enough to peak your interest. If this is the case, then consider the implications over a larger time period with the compound effect. In a 10-year period, Brian Tracy explains that these investments compound and eventually result in a 1004% increase in improvement. Still too tired to get up and invest in a morning routine? Hopefully this inspires you to jump right out of bed and invest in yourself so you can eventually experience a grand of growth that will astonish the people around you because of what you are able to accomplish. If you are not interested at this point, be aware that this same concept can work against you if you are consistently making the wrong decisions on a daily basis.

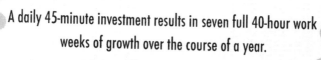

A daily 45-minute investment results in seven full 40-hour work weeks of growth over the course of a year.

-@coytecooper

NO MORE NEGATIVE INTEREST RATES

Have you ever owned a credit card where you made poor decisions and missed payments on an occasional or regular basis? I have to admit that this was something that I did during my college years. It didn't take long for me to learn a valuable lesson. At first I started with smaller payments due and was able to handle parts of them fairly easily. However, as my bank account drew lower, I got lazy and made the decision that it would be all right to miss payments because I would just pay them off in the summer. This ended up being a mistake for two reasons. First, while I didn't know it at the time, it pretty much scorched my credit score and I had to work long and hard to get it back up after college. Second, as I continued to add debt to the card and missed payments, the interest rates started to compound. Over time, the smaller $200 account balance turned into a whopping $5,000 that required me to work long hours all summer to pay off. My lack of discipline and poor daily decision making cost me because I was forced to go in to the next year with very little financial reserves. Fortunately, I learned a valuable lesson about never allowing negative interest rates to compound and dictate my life.

While I made the decision to control the negative compound interest on my credit cards, I did not realize that the concept actually applied to other areas of my life until a much later time. The reality is that this concept is present in our lives every single day. In each moment, we make decisions that are either good or bad. We have already illustrated the compound potential of good decisions in the previous morning routine example. As you have probably already guessed, the same concept holds true for our bad decisions. The only difference is that they can drastically impact our lives in a negative manner. Let's take a very common decision that we make each day in the area of entertainment. Did you know that the average American actually watches television for over three hours a day? While this may not startle you at first, the actual compound number is something that will likely give you pause as you switch on your flat screen tonight to watch your favorite shows. Applying the three-hour statistic, this means that the average American takes in 1,095 hours of television each year, which is the equivalent of 27 full 40-hour workweeks.

This is a staggering amount of time that you spend on messages that often are negative and impact the quality of your mindset and life. Similar to the previous morning routine example, if you make this decision over and over, it is likely that the implications will compound and you will be impacted more by the negative messages as time passes. This is exactly why our society has become so negative and pessimistic. We consistently make decisions that place our minds around negative stimuli (information and people) on a regular basis and this ultimately impacts our daily approach. If you want to improve your effectiveness and chances of success, then you need to be far more diligent about how you spend your time each day. After all, these small, seemingly insignificant decisions will compound over time and eventually drastically influence the quality of life that you experience.

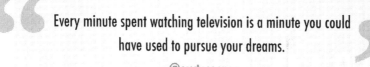

> Every minute spent watching television is a minute you could have used to pursue your dreams.
>
> -@coytecooper

NEGATIVE COMPOUNDING IN ACTION

Maybe the previous television example is not for you. It is possible that you simply don't watch much television or you don't believe that it impacts your life in a significant manner. In either instance, there are all kinds of examples around you every single day on negative decisions and their effects as they compound over time. Let's take a basic health example that influences about 50% of all Americans. Did you know that the average person drinks 1.6 cans of soda each day? On the surface, this seems like a pretty harmless statistic. However, let's examine this situation a little closer to illustrate the influence of the negative compound effect. The number of calories in this amount of soda amounts to approximately 220 calories each day. Again, this by itself does not seem like anything that would drastically impact our life. As a single drink or done occasionally in moderation, it likely would not. However, if you drink it every single day, this number starts to compound and eventually adds up to 80,300 calories throughout the course of a year. Assuming that you have a normal caloric diet otherwise (which may not be a wise assumption here), this single decision made consistently over the course of the year would add up to approximately 23 excess pounds in 365 days. Combine this with other poor dietary habits and a lack of an exercise routine, and you can see why obesity in the United States is at an all-time high. Interestingly, it is this negative compound effect that is at the core of many of our societal issues, and it a primary reason why so many people are unhappy with their lives. If any of these situations apply to you, the good news is that you can do something about it right away if you are willing to change your habits on a daily basis.

WHY DON'T PEOPLE DO SOMETHING ABOUT IT?

When you see the previous example, you are probably wondering why the heck anybody would make this type of decision on a regular basis. If you drink soda consistently, I would be willing to bet you may be rethinking your philosophy on this daily decision. The reason that you are considering making this change is because perhaps you never knew how much this small decision could negatively impact your life over extended periods of time. And this is the exact reason why people continue to make poor decisions on a daily basis. They simply have no idea how their individual daily decisions impact their long-term health, success, and overall effectiveness. The reality in our society is that most people live from moment to moment and rarely give any thought to the consequences of their actions. As explained by leadership expert Jim Rohn, because their actions do not have immediate consequences, they continue to make these decisions consistently until they compound and have dire consequences. Unfortunately, this is the point where most people feel helpless and they continue to make decisions that continue to detract from their quality of life. The key is to recognize the long-term consequences of your decisions in the moment so that you can change behavior. However, it is important to note that this concept does not only apply to our daily routine decisions. There are also applications to the opportunities that we choose to pursue on a daily basis. There are bad, good, and great decisions, and your ability to spend time on ones aligned with your vision can drastically influence the success that you realize in the future.

MOVING FROM GOOD TO GREAT

Not all opportunities are created equal. There are some that are bad and some that are good. Obviously, we want to eliminate bad opportunities because they add no value to what we are pursuing in life. Get in the habit of spotting these opportunities so you can immediately eliminate them from your life. For most people, this is not a difficult decision to make because nobody really wants to spend all of their time on situations that have no chance of enhancing their lives. This is not the reason why most proactive people fail to live their dreams. The most common mistake that these individuals make in their time management is saying yes far too often to good opportunities. For practical purposes, we will define good opportunities as situations that are often intriguing and have the potential to help you advance in some area of your life. This sounds pretty promising, right? Not so fast, because while they may add some value to your life, they are deceiving and considered only good opportunities because they have little to no tie-in to your goals, dreams and vision. As a result, you want to be careful about pursuing these opportunities because they are a lot like fools gold. While they look good on the surface, they will likely never bring you real happiness because they do not contribute to your core purpose. The importance of this process is best illustrated by author and motivational speaker Myles Munroe when discussing vision and opportunities: "My priority is not to get involved in good things; it is to get involved in the right things. Good is not always right. Some people are so preoccupied with good things that they have no time left to do the right thing that they were born to do. The right thing is defined by your purpose." The great opportunities are the ones that inspire us and provide us with energy because they are connected to our purpose. These are ones that align with our areas of genius and allow us to excel and perform at an elite level. The challenge is that you need to become proficient at spotting these great opportunities so you can pursue them with your full attention. This can be quite tricky because they often come disguised as challenges that your intuition initially seeks to avoid. You need to learn to spot these so you can remind yourself that the safe route is rarely the one that will lead you on the path to your dreams.

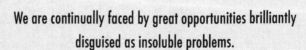

> We are continually faced by great opportunities brilliantly disguised as insoluble problems.
> - Lee Iacocca

Great Opportunities Disguised As Problems

Author and former Chrysler CEO Lee Iacocca explains this about opportunity: "We are continually faced by great opportunities brilliantly disguised as insoluble problems." The key is to truly heed the hidden advice in this statement because it has the potential to drastically influence your ability to realize your vision. Another way of putting this is that most people miss out on great opportunities because we don't even recognize them when they are presented to us.

Instead, they present themselves as challenges and people tend to avoid them because of their propensity to be comfortable. If this statement rings true for you and you are focused on taking the easiest route, then know that you will not recognize great opportunities because they will look like difficult situations that are not worth your time. However, it is important to note that this mindset will make it inevitable that you will miss opportunities that would allow you to stretch yourself and move towards full potential. However, if you change your mindset to embrace situations that take you out of your comfort zone, then you will start to recognize these great opportunities that were previously disguised as insoluble problems. The key is being adamant about embracing challenges so you can progress immediately towards your goals, dreams, and vision on a daily basis. High performers make a habit of taking on big initiatives that other people shy away from because it equips them with a proactive mindset that is a prerequisite for extraordinary accomplishments. Once you start to fully embrace this process, it is essential that you learn to hone the ability to say no to good opportunities so you can spend most of your time on great initiatives that allow you to close the gap on your vision.

It's only by saying no that you can concentrate on the things that are really important.

- Steve Jobs

Learn To Tell People No

Learning to tell people no is one of the most important skill sets you can develop when it comes to pursuing your vision. It also happens to be one of the most difficult to master because turning people down can be an arduous task. Why is this the case? Because we have been conditioned throughout our lives to want people to like us and as a result we often try to do things to please others. The problem with this approach does not lie in doing nice things for others because this is something we should all do every single day. Instead, the issue comes when we say yes to everyone and our days are filled with tasks that do not align with our vision. As a result, we are not being authentic to ourselves and it ends up costing us our ability to focus on what truly matters. The legendary Apple founder Steve Jobs had this to say about success and learning to say no to opportunities: "It comes from saying no to the 1,000 things to make sure we don't get on the wrong track or try to do too much. We're always thinking about new markets we could enter, but it's only by saying no that you can concentrate on the things that are really important." Here is the blunt reality. When we spend our time pleasing others, we rob ourselves of our ability to live our best life and will ultimately end up feeling unsatisfied. If you want to get the opportunity to live your dreams and make your mark on the world, quit making it your central focus to be liked and instead learn to say no to opportunities that do not allow you to progress towards your vision. It would be hard to state this more eloquently than Dr. Stephen Covey in this legendary quote: "You have to decide what your highest priorities are and have the courage - pleasantly, smilingly, nonapologetically - to say 'no' to other things. And the way that you do that is by having a bigger 'yes' burning inside."

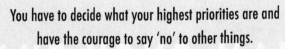

> You have to decide what your highest priorities are and have the courage to say 'no' to other things.
> - Stephen Covey

CLEAR YOUR PLATE

The ability to say no is an essential element to success because it will allow you to clear your plate so you can focus your energy on great opportunities. I have to admit that this is something I have personally struggled with in the past, and continue to struggle with it even now. It is not difficult for me to identify good opportunities that do not align with my vision. However, I have not completely mastered the clear your plate concept because knowing and doing something about it are two very different things. We have already touched on the fact that is it difficult to tell people no because of our propensity to want to be liked. In addition, it is not realistic or smart for most people to simply drop all of their prior commitments without any notice. While you certainly want to allocate your time to high priority activities as soon as possible, sometimes you need to honor your commitments so you can maintain existing strong relationships. With that being said, it is essential that you create a plan to clear your plate in a reasonable time frame so you can focus your attention on initiatives that contribute to your vision. One critical step in this process is paying attention to how you are living your days so you can determine how much of your time is spent on less than great initiatives.

Examine Your Daily Actions

If your vision is going to determine your lifestyle, then it makes sense to assess your current daily actions to determine exactly where you are going to need to make changes. Don't be afraid to acknowledge your shortcomings because we all have areas that we can improve upon to be more efficient with our time. This will allow you to take stock of how well you are currently living your days. Have you made the commitment to get up early and develop yourself so you can reach full potential? When you get up in the morning, is your attitude positive or negative? What do you spend your money on and how do you use your free time? These are all questions that you should ask yourself as you assess how you allocate your time on a daily basis. On top of this, the overarching question you should ask yourself is "are you approaching your day in a manner that will allow you to eventually earn the right to live your dreams?" If the answer here is "no" in any area of your life, then you need to ask yourself how much you want to achieve these dreams. If they are connected to your purpose and a powerful "why," then you will be driven to immediately make changes so you can emphatically say yes to this question. This process may take time to iron out, but it is important that you take steps immediately so you are constantly improving how efficient you are in allocating your time to realizing your aspirations.

> **Successful people are world-class at focusing their time on things that truly matter to their vision.**
>
> -@coytecooper

Focus Sharply on High ROI Areas

The one way you can guarantee that you are always progressing towards your dreams is by being world-class at spending the bulk of your time on high Return on Investment (ROI) areas. These are the smaller, daily initiatives that serve as checkpoint items on the way to achieving your aspirations. From a progression standpoint, these will include the action items that you have determined to be most essential in achieving your one-year goals from earlier in the book. In *Master Your Time, Master Your Life*, Robin Sharma explains that one of the primary things that differentiates the most successful people on the planet from the status quo is that they are diligent about protecting their time. These high performers are disciplined about blocking out distractions so they can be world-class at focusing sharply on activities that will allow them to live to their full potential. It is a subtle shift in mindset that allows them to be far more efficient and productive than most of the people around them on a daily basis. There is nothing flashy about their approach. They are simply world-class at focusing their time on things that truly matter when it comes to their vision. Because they spend most of their time on high priority initiatives that align with their vision, they progress rapidly towards their vision at a rate significantly faster than the normal population.

Take Your "Little Things" To The Top

If you took the time to study highly successful people, you would be amazed at the simplicity in their approach to living. Yet this is exactly what allows them to perform at a high level on a daily basis. The world's most successful people are absolutely adamant about narrowing in on their high ROI areas so they can spend their days progressing towards their vision. They give their most important priorities their full attention so they can perform these activities to the best of their ability consistently each day. As explained by best selling author Jeff Olson, "The successful and the unsuccessful both do the same basic things in their lives, day in and day out. Yet the things successful people do take them to the top, while the things unsuccessful people do take them down and out. So what's the difference? The difference is their awareness, understanding, and applications of the slight edge in their life and work." Successful people take the time to know the activities that will transform their life, and then they have the self-discipline to follow through on them masterfully over extended periods of time until they become world-class habits. There is nothing magical about their approach. It is simply about being willing to embrace the regular application of the fundamentals today that most people neglect and put off until tomorrow.

THE SOMEDAY SYNDROME

One of the biggest mistakes that people commonly make is buying in to the "Someday Syndrome." They tell themselves stories about the things they will achieve in the future. They will lose weight, tomorrow. They will start reading books, next week. They will pursue their dreams, once they have the time to do so. They will take steps to change their lives, someday. The problem with this approach is that someday never comes and they end up with a life that is disappointing. In *The Slight Edge*, author Jeff Olson describes this process: "The problem is that most of us live with one foot planted firmly in the past and the other tucked timidly in the future - never in the moment. In relation to everything - our kids, our health, our home, our career - we tick through the hours in constant regret and Monday morning-quarterbacking about what's behind us, and with worry, anxiety, and dread about what lies ahead." There is no question that the past and the future will play a role in your path to success. However, it is important that you cast them in a limited role when it comes to your daily interactions or you will never get the chance to realize your full potential. The past should be used to learn lessons that will allow you to be more efficient and your vision for the future should provide a framework for your daily actions. Once that is done, you need to spend at least 95 percent of your days getting to work so you can earn the right to live your dreams. Your mind needs to be focused on embracing the precious present if you are going to eventually live your best life and make your mark on the world.

THE PRECIOUS PRESENT

In Spencer Johnson's *The Precious Present*, he tells a story of a young boy who meets with an old man and learns about a precious gift. The old man refers to it as "The Precious Present" and explains to him that it is the best gift he can receive because it will allow him to be happy forever. Intrigued, the boy goes out on a journey to find this gift, but continues to come back to the old man frustrated because of his lack of ability to find this treasure. After years and years of searching, he returns to the old man agitated and ready to give up on his journey. Finding that the old man was extremely weak and unable to talk, he immediately grew frightened that he would never be able to find this precious present. Fatigued by his situation, he decided to stop trying and immediately had an insight into what the old man was referring to. It had never had anything to do with wishes or an end destination that occupies your mind all day long. No, it was far more simple than that. It was not the past and not the future. It was about being present in each moment with an attitude of gratitude for the gifts in your life. He was not able to see it because he was too preoccupied with the future and some grand end destination. "The Precious Present" that the old man had mentioned had been available to him all along, but he had just been too distracted to see it.

The previous tale is one that most of us can relate to because it is something that we have all experienced in our lives. As Monday rolls around, we are already thinking about the next weekend because we intuitively believe that it is what we need to be happy. Or, we may be spending our days pondering a vacation that is months away because we have trained our mind to be unhappy with the mundane activities that make up our days. You may even be dreaming about retirement and all the things you will be able to do when you no longer have to work. We all have things like this that we wish for because we believe that these end destinations will provide us with happiness. Former First Lady Barbara Bush had this to say about this approach: "We get onboard that train at birth, and we want to cross the continent because we have in mind that somewhere out there is a station. We pass by cities and factories, but we don't look at any of it because we want to get to the station. This station changes for us during life. To begin with, for most of us it's turning 18, getting out of high school. Then the station is that first promotion, and then the station becomes getting the kids out of college, and then the station becomes retirement, and then... all too late we recognize this truth... there really isn't a station. The joy is in the journey, and the journey is the joy." We have failed to recognize the true gift of the precious present when we skip our daily moments looking for the next big thing. Because we are always spending our days dreaming about something in the future, we miss out on amazing moments in front of us that could be truly remarkable. If your mind is always in the future, it is impossible to make the smaller investments consistently that are required for you to live your dreams. Become a person who enjoys the precious present so you can realize your full potential and live your best life.

> Successful people maintain a positive focus in life no matter what is going on around them.
> -@JackCanfield

BLOCK OUT THE UNNECESSARY NOISE

If there is one thing that you should take from this chapter, it is that the choices you make every single day matter. That, and you are in complete control of every one of them. If you want to elevate your life, then you must choose to invest in high ROI initiatives that will guarantee you progress towards your goals. One step you can make to leverage the compound effect and to drastically transform your life is to get up each morning to go through a simple growth routine. Once you have done this and started your day in a productive manner, you can assess how you are spending your time and say no to the initiatives and opportunities that are not in alignment with your vision. Beyond this, you should be adamant about eliminating thoughts, activities, and people who slow you from progressing towards your goals and dreams. It is essential that you learn to block out any negativity that does not align with the person you would like to become in the future. If someone constantly laughs at your dreams and/or often criticizes your aspirations, then you may need to remove them from your life completely. In these instances, remember this advice from Jack Canfield, co-author of the Chicken Soup for the Soul series: "Successful people maintain a positive focus in life no matter what is going on around them. They stay focused on their past successes rather than their past failures, and on the next action steps they need to take to get them closer to the fulfillment on their goals rather than all of the other distractions that life presents them." It is important to point out that this concept is easier said than done because it is difficult to learn to block out the unnecessary noise around you. It takes discipline to regularly assess your environment so you are able to identify areas that are not a productive part of the pursuit of your vision. And once you know these areas, it takes boldness to be willing to tell people no and to remove them from your life when necessary. These are simply costs that you must pay to earn the right to live your dreams. It is your job to determine whether you are willing to make this sacrifice. However, remind yourself that no great accomplishments in life are easy to achieve, and you must be willing to pay the price every single day to make them a reality.

JEFF OLSON

Jeff Olson is the author of the bestselling book *The Slight Edge*, owner of the Live Happy magazine, and Founder and CEO of Nerium International. He has impacted hundreds of thousands of lives across the United States and the world and he continues to find new ways to make his mark on the world. However, this was not always the case for him as he explained in his book that he was at one point a "beach bum." After realizing that he had more potential inside him, he set out to become an entrepreneur and was successful at building a highly effective company. However, the company eventually came upon hard times and he ended up going out of business. Committed to realizing his full potential, he reflected on his performance and realized his success and failures all came back to the ability to embrace little things that gave him a slight edge advantage. When he was successful, he was outstanding at implementing productive daily actions consistently over time that compounded and allowed him to perform at an elite level. When he failed, he had simply neglected these habits and the slight edge worked in the opposite direction. With this knowledge, he set out again committed to building a successful business career and to inspire others to make daily decisions that will transform their lives. The end result of his ability to block out clutter and focus on activities that truly matter has been a unique ability to make a lasting impression on people's lives across the world.

KEY SUMMARY POINTS

○   Life is designed to be simple. When your vision is crystal clear, it will help you to achieve simplicity in your approach because it will guide all of your decisions on a daily basis.

○   Striving for small 1/1000th daily gains is the most effective route to success. Making the right investments consistently over extended periods will allow your efforts to compound and you will eventually experience one grand of growth.

○   Learning to tell people no is an important step for clearing your plate so you are able to focus on high priority ROI areas that are essential to your vision.

○   Be careful about falling victim to the "Someday Syndrome." Rather than sitting around waiting for the ideal environment, get to work today implementing action items that are essential for reaching your goals.

CHAPTER 8

FAIL FORWARD AND LEARN FROM REPETITION

> Don't dwell on what went wrong. Instead, focus on what to do next. Spend your energies on moving forward toward finding the answer.
>
> - Denis Waitley

IT WAS THE last match of my college wrestling career and I walked off the mat dejected. While I had earned All-American status, I had failed in my pursuit to become a National Champion. In my mind at the time, this meant that I was a failure. As I left the arena with my family, my brain was filled with a variety of emotions that left me mentally drained. Anyone who has failed in this capacity knows that one immediate reaction is to question the time and energy that was invested in the pursuit. It had to be a waste of time given that you did not reach your end destination, right? Actually, this is wrong because there are a variety of benefits that can result from failure, and life is an ongoing process where your failures eventually provide you with an opportunity to succeed in an extraordinary manner if you handle them properly. But you must be willing to change your mindset so you see failure as a part of the path to success. You must approach each situation that you face whether good or bad as an opportunity to grow and move towards full potential. This is where a proactive growth mindset comes in to play.

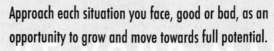

> Approach each situation you face, good or bad, as an opportunity to grow and move towards full potential.
> -@coytecooper

THE FIXED V GROWTH MINDSETS

In Carol Dweck's *Mindset*, she touches on two different mindsets that she has encountered in her research as a psychologist: the growth mindset and the fixed mindset. In the fixed mindset, people tend to believe that their abilities and skills are set and there is nothing they can do about it. As a result, they are far less likely to take risks and to get out of their comfort zone because they will associate any initiatives that fall short of expectations as a failure. With a fixed mindset, they truly believe that this effort directly reflects both their abilities and skill sets. This leads them to see themselves as a failure and they are far more likely to withdraw and avoid risks that threaten their position. Unfortunately, this also results in them never being able to reach their full potential because they are not willing to step out of their comfort zone and embrace learning from the process. If you want to achieve meaningful success, you must avoid this fixed mindset, as it will severely limit your growth and ability to progress towards aspirations.

On the flip side, people with a growth mindset tend to proactively perceive each situation as an opportunity to learn. When presented with a challenge, they are excited to take it head on because they know they will progress towards their vision regardless of the outcome. As explained by Dweck, "The growth mindset is based on the belief that your basic qualities are things you can cultivate through your efforts. Although people may differ in every which way - in their initial talents and aptitudes, interests, or temperaments - everyone can change and grow through application and experience." People with a growth mindset see all situations as an opportunity to grow, and because they do not fear failure, they are far more likely to get out of their comfort zone and pursue their dreams. Falling short of expectations is not something that they take personally. Instead, it is simply a small stumble on the path to achieve extraordinary accomplishments. Their ability to embrace repetition makes them a prime candidate for success because they understand that adversity is a necessary component for realizing lofty aspirations.

THE REAL FORMULA FOR SUCCESS

If I were to ask you the secret to success, what would you say? When asking audiences, some of the most common responses are increasing your workload, cultivating unique skill sets, and/or improving your quality connections in life. While these are sound answers that would not necessarily be incorrect, there is an answer that is far more effective that may catch you off guard a little. When asked about the secret formula for success, IBM founder Thomas J. Watson explained the following: "It's quite simple, really. Double your rate of failure. You're thinking of failure as the enemy of success. But it isn't at all... you can be discouraged from failure - or you can learn from it. So go ahead and make mistakes. Make all you can. Because, remember that's where you will find success. On the far side." The fascinating thing about our society is that most people believe that success is avoiding failure and protecting our status. This is a common perception that often robs people of the ability to take risks and to learn from the process. If you want to be successful and reach your full potential, you must train your mind to embrace a proactive "Fail Forward" mindset.

> ## If you want to be successful, double your rate of failure.
> — Thomas J. Watson

THE "FAIL FORWARD" MENTALITY

If you have a fixed mindset, the "Fail Forward" concept that will be presented in this section might sound truly absurd to you. Who would really want to approach each situation seeking out failure? The real answer here is no one. Even people with a growth mindset don't go in to their days hoping they will fail at key initiatives. Their full intention is to work hard and to succeed when they are presented with opportunities to demonstrate their skill sets. However, they also understand that their lofty aspirations will require them to live way outside their comfort zone to make them a reality. There is simply no way they can reach their "unreasonable" dreams if they do not commit to the type of actions that stretch them to reach their full potential. While they may not recognize it, they have embraced a mindset that growth expert Dr. John Maxwell refers to as the "Fail Forward" mentality and he explains this about the approach: "Failing forward is the ability to get back up after you've been knocked down, learn from your mistake, and move forward in a better direction." In these instances, the quicker the better so you can improve your abilities and skill sets with each repetition.

As we have learned from IBM founder Thomas J. Watson, failure is a part of the process when you have lofty aspirations and high expectations. Big dreams demand that you step way out of your comfort zone to grow and make them a reality. It is never your job to avoid failure because it is inevitable if you are committed to pursuing your vision with a passion. The key is resiliency and being a quick learner when you fall short of expectations so you can capitalize on the process of repetition. With each one that you actively pursue, you have an opportunity to learn lessons that can launch you towards your desired end destination. When you commit to consistently learning from the process and remain steadfast in your pursuit of excellence, it is inevitable that you will give yourself a chance to realize full potential. This approach will eventually put you in a rare group of individuals who get the opportunity to live their dreams. Who knew that failure was the key to success? Commit to failing forward today friends!

Big dreams demand that you step way out of your comfort
zone to grow and make them a reality.

-@coytecooper

THE GIFT OF THE GROWTH MINDSET

We have already established the fact that I had a fixed mindset when competing as a college wrestler. We have also made it clear that there were consequences to this approach as I was not able to reach my full potential. The important thing to recognize is that a fixed mindset is not something that is set in stone. In fact, you can change this mentality instantly if you truly recognize the limitations in your current approach and commit to seeing every opportunity you face as one where you can grow and improve your skill sets. While it may take time and effort to fully adopt a growth mindset in all areas of your life, you will start to see immediate benefits when you are willing to take risks and live outside of your comfort zone.

Another positive aspect of embracing a growth mindset is that it allows you to retroactively learn lessons from past "failures." This subtle shift in your approach will provide clarity in previous blind spots that you were not able to recognize while in a fixed mindset. While you cannot change the outcomes of your past, you can learn from them and use the lessons to have a far more productive future. They can serve as consistent reminders to embrace stepping out of your comfort zone and to pursue lofty aspirations. In the words of American actor, writer, and director Woody Allen, "If you don't fail now and again, it's a sign you're playing it safe." There is nothing devastating or even disappointing about putting in extraordinary efforts and falling short of expectations. When you are in a growth, "Fail Forward" mindset, these are simply situations that present an opportunity to learn and move towards full potential. Eventually, this approach and mindset will make it inevitable that you achieve unique accomplishments that allow you to make your mark on the world.

> If you don't fail now and again, it's a sign you're playing it safe.
> - Woody Allen

LESSONS LEARNED FROM FALLING SHORT

While I did not recognize the lessons being presented in my college wrestling career in real time, I can now acknowledge them as critical moments in my life that have shaped me as a person. It is important to point out that I was not able to diagnose these lessons until I learned to embrace a growth mindset way after the fact. The interesting thing is this single pursuit that I initially deemed as a complete failure has taught me as much about success than virtually any other situation in my life. I now realize that this is fitting given the role that falling short of expectations plays in success when you are committed to "failing forward" and living outside of your comfort zone. The lessons I have learned from not realizing my dreams as a college wrestler have impacted how I now approach each day as I strive to reach my full potential and to make my mark on the world. But I had to be ready to see these lessons for them to be an asset in my pursuit to live my dreams.

LESSON #1: THE FEAR OF FAILURE GUARANTEES MEDIOCRITY.

The first thing I learned from my shortcomings as a college wrestler is that the fear of failure pretty much ensures that you will never realize your full potential. Somewhere in my transition from high school to college, I had a subtle shift in my mindset where I focused on trying not to lose rather than striving to grow and perform at a peak level. You get the difference in this approach, right? I definitely did not at the time, but I now fully recognize that I shifted to a fixed mindset that ultimately limited my ability to progress towards my dreams and goals. Rather than being grateful for the opportunity to compete, I started to become afraid of failing because I tended to take it too personally. When I approached my matches, I remember being worried about losing and this caused me to play it safe in my offensive approach. When skill sets were comparable, the end result was that I lost to opponents who had a growth mindset. The good news is that this taught me a valuable lesson for life. If you want to reach your absolute full potential, you must shift to a growth mindset so you can embrace opportunities that allow you to progress.

LESSON #2: DWELLING ON FAILURE LIMITS ABILITY TO LEARN.

Another common mistake in my college wrestling career that came from having a fixed mindset was getting too caught up in losses. Being worried about the perception of "failure," I often spent days beating myself up over losses. I overanalyzed my performance and worried about what it would look like to the people around me. The reality is that most people probably were not even paying that much attention to my performance because they had lives to live. With a growth mindset, I would have known to immediately look for the opportunities to improve following matches because this would have been the quickest route to reaching my goals. This is something that I now embrace daily in my pursuit to reach full potential. Rather than dwell on situations where I fall short of expectations, I now pride myself on failing forward as quickly as possible. With each repetition, I know that I am one step closer to living my dreams.

> With each failure, you are presented with another opportunity to move one step closer to your dreams.
> -@coytecooper

LESSON #3: AN "OLLIN" APPROACH IS A PREREQUISITE FOR SUCCESS. When it comes to pursuing your lofty vision, there is no success to be found when you have a timid approach. No easy route, remember? If you want to get the opportunity to live your dreams, you must do everything in your power to make sure that your level of action and commitment are at least in alignment with your high expectations. This requires that you adopt an approach where you go "Ollin" and live outside of your comfort zone so you have the opportunity to progress towards your vision. With this approach, you cannot allow yourself to have an outlet to let yourself off the hook when things get challenging. There is no room for excuses or you will likely use them at the first opportunity when your environment is less than ideal. When your vision is clear, the key is to make it an essential priority to pursue it with your full attention until it becomes a reality.

It's Never A Waste Of Time

Remember when I mentioned that an initial common response when falling short of expectations is to question the time and energy investment? If you have ever pursued a dream with your full attention, this is likely something that you can understand because it is not fun to fail in any meaningful endeavor. This is particularly true when you work extremely hard and believe that you deserve to succeed. Life does not always give you what you think you deserve and there will come a time when adversity shows up at your front doorstep. When this time comes, it is important that you remind yourself of the importance of the growth mindset. If you go "Ollin" to pursue a goal and/or dream, it is never a waste of time. While you may not have the opportunity to realize the exact aspiration that you are after, there is always a valuable lesson to be learned from your situation if you have the right perspective. Interestingly, our society seems to place such a high value on winning (and being the best) that we often feel like a failure when we are not the best at what we do. Yet there is always value to be found in pursuing initiatives to the best of our abilities. If we perform to our full potential and fall short of expectations, then we can always live with the outcome. This is an instance where we get the most out of ourselves and the only thing to do at this point is to reflect and strive to improve for future opportunities. While you fell short of expectations, this is a situation you can call a quality repetition. Get enough of these and you will eventually have the chance to achieve some remarkable accomplishments.

You Are Guaranteed Nothing

Lots of motivational speakers tout the fact that you can achieve anything you set your mind to achieving. While this sounds great, it is not always realistic. The reality is that you likely will not become an NBA All-Star if you are 5'1" and lack athletic ability. This would be an instance of having a dream that is not in alignment with your purpose and area(s) of genius. It is certainly possible for you to improve your skill sets and become an effective player, but it is not likely that you will realize your dream. This is why it is so important that you choose aspirations that are in alignment with your gifts and passion. When you do this, you give yourself the best chance of realizing your dreams if you have the right mindset and are willing to earn it each day over extended periods of time. This will include failing forward and being willing to embrace adversity as part of the process. If you do these things right, you give yourself the best opportunity to live your dreams.

IMPERFECT ACTION IS BETTER THAN PERFECT STAGNATION

One of the most common reasons that people never get the chance to realize their dreams and reach full potential is that they fail to act on their intentions. This is something we have alluded to in this book. At some point, most people have aspirations that they get excited about pursuing and have every intention of making them a reality. If all motivational speakers were correct, it would seem that this would be enough to guarantee success as they are often fully convinced that they are going to make things happen in their minds. Yet when you study intentions, it doesn't take long to realize that very few people actually do what it takes to make their goals a reality. While there are a variety of reasons why this may be the case, one of the biggest obstacles is the misperception that you need the ideal environment to get started. Equally limiting is the expectation that initial steps need to be perfect when pursuing aspirations. This is not a realistic expectation and it causes people to fail to take action. It does not take a genius to recognize that you cannot achieve your dreams if you are not willing to take steps to make them a reality. The overarching lesson here is that imperfect action is much better than perfect stagnation. Rather than worrying about being perfect, get out and embrace the opportunity to get quality repetitions that will allow you to fail yourself to the top. "Don't worry about failures," explained author and motivational speaker Jack Canfield. "Worry about the chances you miss when you don't even try."

> Don't worry about failures. Worry about the chances you miss when you don't even try.
> -@JackCanfield

FIND 10,000 WAYS THAT DON'T WORK

Repetition is how you learn. If you want to be a great public speaker, then you need to put yourself in a position to get in front of audiences to deliver messages on a regular basis. This often includes intentionally inserting yourself into positions that are uncomfortable where you will inevitably fall short at some point. If you make a habit of living outside your comfort zone, the opportunity will present itself to learn from situations where you do not perform to expectations. As others are avoiding "failure" at all costs, you place yourself in a position to differentiate your skill sets because you are willing to embrace uncomfortable situations that few other people are willing to face. You are welcoming a process conducive to growth because you are taking advantage of productive repetitions. Remind yourself in these situations that you have not failed at all when you fall short of expectations.

Rather, you have simply encountered a situation where you have the opportunity to learn lessons that have fostered some of the greatest achievements our world has ever seen. For this to occur, you will have to embrace the "Fail Forward" mindset illustrated by Thomas Edison in this legendary quote: "I have not failed. I've just found 10,000 ways that won't work." Not 10,000 failures. 10,000 quality repetitions that eventually allowed him to invent the light bulb. It was the process of knowing all the ways that wouldn't work that allowed Edison to eventually find what would work. Are you willing to make that type of investment to live your dreams?

> " I have not failed. I've just found 10,000 ways that won't work. "
> - Thomas Edison

FAILING OVER AND OVER AGAIN

Thomas Edison is not the only one who has embraced the "fail forward" mentality as an essential part of success. This is the case for virtually any person who has accomplished something truly unique in their life. Most people would consider Michael Jordan as one of the greatest athletes to ever grace this planet. However, the mistake that people often make when idolizing Jordan is that they see him as a perfect athlete who is immune to failures. This could not be further from the truth. When you study his career, you actually find that he was able to succeed in an extraordinary manner because of his tolerance to put himself in positions where he fell short of expectations. If you don't believe me, then listen to what he had to say about his rise to success: "I've missed more than 9,000 shots in my career. I've lost almost 300 games. 26 times I've been trusted to take the game winning shot and missed. I've failed over and over and over again in my life. And that is why I succeed." It is no accident that Michael Jordan is seen as one of the greatest competitors we have ever seen in the sports arena. He was so passionate about his vision that he was willing to "fail forward" to reach his end destination.

> " I've failed over and over and over again in my life. And that is why I succeed. "
> - Michael Jordan

The Only True Failure

We have already touched on the fact that a fear of failure is common in our society. We are so consumed with what we look like to others that we often avoid situations that will portray us as anything other than being perfect. Interestingly, this is the one way that failure is inevitable. You see, the only true failure in life is when we waste our talents and do nothing to realize our full potential. Billionaire and author of the best selling Harry Potter series J.K. Rowling had this to say about living within our comfort zone: "You might never fail on the scale that I did, but some failure in life is inevitable. It is impossible to live without failing at something, unless you live so cautiously that you might as well not lived at all - in which case, you fail by default." The sad thing is that most people choose to live cautiously to protect their image. They have no idea this exact approach is guiding them directly to failure, and this will eventually lead to regrets later in life about the path they did not take to realize their full potential.

Fail Your Way To Success In The Future

It's time to get moving on failing your way to success. Hopefully we have done enough for you to understand the importance of embracing this philosophy and now it is time to take action. As with all of the other concepts presented in the book, while you are excited about embracing them in your life, sometimes it can be difficult to determine how to get started. It is essential that you remind yourself that the most important thing is that you commit to taking action immediately. It does not need to be perfect, remember? Instead, make a decision to do something today to embrace a mindset where failure is a part of the process. Building on the concepts outlined in the chapter, here are some steps that you can take to get on the path to failing forward towards your dreams.

1. LEARN TO LIVE OUTSIDE COMFORT ZONE. When it comes to success and making your mark on the world, one of the most effective strategies you can implement is embracing a mindset where you commit to living outside of your comfort zone. Your gifts must be cultivated to reach full potential and the only way to ensure this happens is by doing things that challenge you. While this often goes against conventional thinking in our society, it is always within your power to extend your comfort zone by regularly embracing situations that make you uncomfortable. When you adopt a growth mindset, you will be far more likely to face situations that give you anxiety because you know this is exactly what you need to do to turn them into strengths. This is an important step in the growth process because it will allow you to stop avoiding high priority opportunities that make you uncomfortable. Eventually, these exact situations will be ones that you look forward to because your growth mindset will allow you to turn them into valuable skill sets. The first step is to determine that you are committed to living outside of your comfort zone so you can eventually realize your full potential and live all of your dreams.

2. TRAIN YOUR BRAIN TO LOVE "NO'S". This will be another concept that will likely be counterintuitive to what you have been taught in your life. Building on the concept of doubling your rate of failure, best selling author and speaker Brian Tracy emphasizes the importance of re-wiring your brain to look forward to receiving "no's." While he introduces this concept in the context of excelling in the area of sales, the lesson is applicable to all situations in life where you need to receive a yes to realize your dreams. In these instances, he explains that you can actually train your mind to be excited about getting "no's." Rather than seeing them as a rejection, you can focus on the fact that each no that you receive provides an opportunity to learn from the process. With each repetition, you can develop skill sets that will allow you to move one step closer to realizing your dreams. It is a process that often takes time to cultivate, but you can train your brain to embrace rejections. However, let me be clear about exactly what I mean here. It is important to note that you never approach a challenge with the sole intention of underperforming and getting a no response. This would defeat the purpose of the entire process. Instead, you are approaching each situation with the intention of performing to the best of your abilities. When you fall short of expectations, the key is to never take it too personally. In these instances, you simply learn from the situation and commit to improving your abilities so you eventually get the yes that you desire.

3. BE QUICK AT FINDING THE LESSON. Even when you are determined to fail forward, there are going to be times when falling short of expectations causes you to dwell on the outcome. In these instances, do not beat yourself up for your shortcomings. Instead, remind yourself of the importance of failing forward and all of the concepts presented in this chapter. At this point, it is time to teach yourself to be quick at finding the lesson in the situation you are facing. This is exactly the time that you need to focus on the growth mindset and flipping the script on negative thoughts. Rather than dwell on what you did not accomplish, focus sharply on areas where you can improve and develop a plan of attack that allows you to reach full potential moving forward. If you are an athlete and just lost a game or match, move on quickly from making it personal and instead identify areas of your performance you can enhance immediately to increase the chances of success in your upcoming competitions. If you have been working hard to get a promotion and are denied the opportunity, resist the urge to place the blame on others and instead focus on how you can improve so you are more likely to elevate your professional standing in the future. It is essential that you close the gap on the time from when you fall short of expectations and when you do something proactive to make it a positive experience. If you can accomplish this task and quickly move on to areas of improvement, you will capitalize on repetition and differentiate yourself from other people who dwell on negative situations.

TIME TO FAIL FORWARD!

You now understand that success is not about being perfect. Nor is it about intentionally avoiding situations that present a risk of falling short of expectations. These are both approaches that fall under a fixed mindset and will encourage you to do whatever is necessary to live within your comfort zone. The problem with this approach is that it will never allow you to challenge yourself in a way that stretches you and cultivates your area(s) of genius. Not surprisingly, this also ensures that you never reach full potential and get the chance to make your mark on the world. If you want to achieve extraordinary accomplishments and make your life memorable, you need to learn to live outside of your comfort zone on a regular basis. Never avoid situations simply because they make you uncomfortable. These are the exact times you need to step up so you can eventually turn these areas into valuable skill sets. Along with getting accustomed to living outside of your comfort zone, look to embrace the concept of doubling your rate of failure so you can capitalize on quality repetitions that compound your learning. If you can combine a passion to perform at your full potential with a mindset where you are constantly looking to maximize growth, you will be well on your way to earning the right to live your dreams and to make your mark on the world.

> If you want to achieve great things, take action
> immediately and learn from failure.
>
> -@coytecooper

THE MAKE YOUR MARK MASTER

J.K. ROWLING

When you hear the name J.K. Rowling, most people tend to think of a highly talented author who has churned out the Harry Potter series. Being a self-made billionaire, it seems natural to assume that she has unparalleled talents and that everything has come easily to her. This assumption is undeniably false. In a Harvard commencement address, Rowling explained that in the seven years following her graduation she failed on an epic scale. In this time frame, she faced a divorce with her husband, had no job, and was as poor as possible without being homeless in modern Britain. While this situation seems like it would be a cruel punishment with little redeeming value, Rowling explained that this was a turning point in her life. She had hit rock bottom and learned that she could handle it. After all, she still had a daughter that she adored despite all the adversity in her life. With this being the case, she set out with her typewriter and a great idea to achieve something truly extraordinary. Rowling kept this lesson in failure in mind as she went on to write seven books in the Harry Potter book series, which sold hundreds of millions of copies. This led her to become one of the few self-made billionaires in the world. She explained that "Failure gave me an inner security that I had never attained by passing exams. Failure taught me things about myself that I could have learned no other way. I discovered that I had a strong will, and more discipline than I ever expected." It was failure that led Rowling to becoming one of the most successful authors of all time and having the opportunity to make her own unique mark on the world.

KEY SUMMARY POINTS

O   It is impossible to reach your full potential if you are afraid of failure. Adopt a growth mindset where you focus on embracing opportunities that take you out of your comfort zone. When you constantly look for the lessons in each situation and commit to constant improvement, you will be on your way to realizing your goals and full potential.

O   The key to realizing success is to adopt a "fail forward" mentality. While you should never intentionally look to fall short of your expectations, it is essential that you seek out opportunities that take you way out of your comfort zone. When you have lofty aspirations, it is inevitable that you will face failures in your pursuit to reach full potential. You must embrace these situations as opportunities to grow.

O   Thomas Edison did not fail 10,000 times in his pursuit to create the light bulb. Instead, he found 10,000 ways that did not work that were essential lessons for finding the one way that would work. If you want to be successful, you must seek out opportunities to grow regardless of their outcome.

O   Strive to fail your way to success. Commit to living outside of your comfort zone, train your brain to love "no's", and be quick at finding the lesson in situations where you fall short of expectations. Your ability to seek out challenging situations and learn from quality repetitions will determine your ability to realize your dreams and to live your best life.

CHAPTER 9

FLIP THE SCRIPT ON THE "80/20 RULE OF NEGATIVITY"

> If you don't want to get into positive thinking, that's okay. Just
> eliminate all the negative thoughts from your mind,
> and whatever's left will be fine.
> - Bob Rotella, Sports Psychologist

IT WAS A winter afternoon and I was in the process of writing my first book entitled *Impressions* and felt compelled to do research on the importance of having an optimistic outlook. As I was searching through articles on the prominence of positive attitude, I came upon a statistic that completely caught me off guard. If I were to ask you what percentage of our thoughts are positive on a daily basis, what would you guess? Feeling on the optimistic side, maybe you would respond with a favorable 80 percent. Or, you might be a little reserved because the nature of the question and settle with an answer closer to 50 percent. It's also possible you are far more intelligent that I give you credit for and you respond with a confident answer of 20 percent. Well, that or you have read the entire book and were instantly thinking I forgot about the previous example. I assure you that I did not. It just seemed

196 COYTE COOPER, PH.D.

more appropriate to roll it out in a suspenseful manner. Based on this "80/20 Rule of Negativity" (80 percent of thoughts being negative and 20 being positive), this means that the equivalent of almost 195 full days in a single year are occupied by negative thoughts. Did that statistic just blow your mind? It sure did mine when I did the calculation on it. Let's take a look at this from an individual, moment-by-moment perspective to really help the magnitude of this information sink in.

Transitioning This To Individual Thoughts

The Laboratory of Neuro Imagining at the University of Southern California (USC) determined that the average person has 48.6 thoughts a minute. Our mind is truly an active unit that is constantly on the move. Unfortunately, we have conditioned it to be on the move acting on the wrong things. Using the 80/20 ratio as a benchmark, this research by USC scholars would mean that the average human has over 30 negative thoughts per minute. It does not take a math wizard to recognize that this means we have a negative thought flashing through our mind every two seconds. It is important to note that many of these thoughts are subconscious and below the surface so you won't necessarily even know when they are happening, but the outcome is the same because it influences your ability to progress towards your goals. When considering that your mind is not able to hold two thoughts simultaneously, these findings have dire consequences on our ability to advance and achieve success. Every single thought and minute spent on the negative is a thought and minute that could have been spent on productively pursuing our dreams. If you are skeptical about this research on the frequency of unproductive thoughts, simply spend time during an upcoming day being cognizant of your negative thoughts.

S INEVITABLE. PURSUE THE THING YOU ARE MEANT TO DO ALL OUT AND MAKING YOUR MARK IS INEVITABLE. PUR

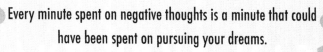

> **Every minute spent on negative thoughts is a minute that could have been spent on pursuing your dreams.**
> -@coytecooper

TAKING TIME TO TRACK YOUR THOUGHTS

It is normal for people's first response to be that of skepticism when they hear this data on negative thoughts. After all, most people have trained their minds to be negative and your immediate response to this information will reflect this habit. As you mull over this information, keep in mind that it is based on the average and may not completely mirror your current situation. It is possible that you are optimistic and your thoughts are more favorable than the data portrays. However, I warn you about completely dismissing this information because I consider myself to be a highly optimistic person and was blown away when I paid closer attention to my thoughts throughout my days. I highly recommend that you do the same so you gain an understanding of how much of your thoughts are wasted on unproductive topics. This is a simple process in which you start with a 30-minute period where you assess your thoughts and make note of the times where you have a negative response. It is important to point out that this initial assessment may be biased because you will likely unconsciously adjust your thoughts to make them seem more favorable. However, even in this case, it is probable that you will still find that you have far more negative thoughts than you ever imagined. The key here is to acknowledge the frequency of these thoughts so you can learn to retrain your brain to focus on the positive. Awareness is one of the first steps to flipping the script on these negative thoughts. After all, it is difficult to change something that you don't acknowledge as being a problem. To further help inspire you to take immediate action, we will explore the implications of negativity so you know exactly what is at stake when you allow the wrong types of thoughts to occupy your mind for extended periods of time.

THE "NOT-SO-GOOD" SIDE EFFECTS OF NEGATIVITY

We do not want to spend too much time on negativity because it would be counterproductive to what we are trying to achieve with this chapter. The goal is to flip the script and this will take a proactive approach. However, with that being said, it is essential that you gain an understanding of the side effects of negativity so you are clear on why you should never allow counter productive thoughts to camp out in your mind. Research has shown that negative thoughts trigger a human's stress response, much like an actual external threat does. This often results in feelings of being afraid, insecure, depressed, and/or anxious. Unfortunately, each of these are associated with undesirable health issues such as a depleted immune system (which results in susceptibility to illness), heart disease, lung problems, and a variety of different unfavorable outcomes. On top of this, negativity has been shown to cloud your judgment and put you in situations where you make poor decisions. From a practical standpoint, there is a very simple consequence that is potentially more important than any of the previous outcomes mentioned. For every minute you spend on negative thoughts, you are robbed of a minute that could have been spent on pursuing your dreams. The bottom line is that negative thoughts do nothing to improve the quality of your life and should be replaced regardless of the cost.

> When you are grateful, fear disappears and abundance appears.
> -@TonyRobbins

THE HAPPINESS ADVANTAGE

The good news is that you can virtually eliminate all of the side effects previously mentioned by simply cultivating a proactive mindset that focuses on the positive. The moment you are in a state of gratitude, you no longer have room for feelings of fear, insecurity, depression, or anxiety. As eloquently stated by Anthony Robbins, "When you are grateful, fear disappears and abundance appears." And with abundance come a variety of benefits that are worth pursuing. Among them is the ultimate feeling of happiness that eludes so many people in our society. In *The Happiness Advantage*, author Shawn Achor explains that studies have demonstrated that happy people are far more creative and they are able to find solutions to problems at a much quicker rate. Research has also been clear about the fact that success is not the cause of happiness. Simply put, earning more money or advancing in your career is not a guarantee that you will be happy. However, top scholars have demonstrated that happy people are far more likely to realize and sustain success than people who are unhappy. The key to making this happiness advantage a reality is retraining your brain to focus on the positive.

CROWD OUT THE NEGATIVE

The opening quote in this chapter is ideal for flipping the script for a couple of reasons. For one, sometimes people have a negative response to positive thinking because of the way it is often positioned by some motivational speakers. For these individuals, this is a very unique way of thinking that makes positive thinking less threatening. In the words of psychologist Bob Rotella, if you don't like positive thinking, simply "eliminate all the negative thoughts from your mind, and whatever's left will be fine." Interestingly, this is a major part of cultivating a positive mindset because one of the keys to making this happen is crowding out the negative. In essence, this refers to being so active about filling your day with the right activities that there is no room for unproductive thoughts. This chapter is all about providing you with a simple structure that will allow you to retrain your brain and flip the script on negative thoughts.

Retraining Your Brain Activities

We have already touched on how difficult it is to achieve lofty aspirations. Because you have set them properly, it is going to take a significant effort on your part to make them a reality in the future. This means that you need to do everything in your power to give yourself an advantage so you can progress efficiently towards your full potential. Given that you have established your unproductive tendencies over long periods of time, it is important that you are realistic in your expectations of what it will take to replace these negative thoughts with more productive habits. If you start with this understanding, you will be far more likely to eventually succeed in your efforts because you will increase your chances of following through when you fall short of expectations. The essential thing is that you must be adamant about not allowing negativity to remain in your life. Once you have made this decision, you can start flipping the script by focusing on seven simple Retrain Your Brain (RYB) Activities. Let's outline these initiatives now so you can get to work transforming your approach.

> If you want to live your dreams, you must be adamant about not allowing negativity to remain in your life.
> -@coytecooper

RYB #1: ACKNOWLEDGING THE NEGATIVE. Nothing will change with your attitude if you are not willing to acknowledge your shortcomings.

Every person on this earth has negative thoughts. The difference with highly successful people is they are proactive about picking them out like weeds so they can create space for their dreams to flourish. This process is impossible to accomplish if you do not train your mind to acknowledge when you have unproductive thoughts. Let's draw back a little bit because it is possible that you are unsure what this even looks like. Driving in traffic when someone suddenly pulls in front of you and cuts you off, it is highly likely that you have responded at some point with frustration and/or anger. Negative. Sitting around judging others on their shortfalls for no particular reason. Negative. Focusing sharply on the challenges around you and how difficult they are going to be to overcome. Negative. There are literally hundreds, if not thousands, of common examples just like this that we have on a daily basis. The first step for you to flip the script on negative thoughts is to acknowledge when you have these types of unproductive thoughts that do not align with your vision. This will allow you to segue into the next Retrain Your Brain (RYB) activity where you sub these thoughts out for more productive ones.

RYB #2: IMMEDIATELY "SUB OUT" FOR MORE PRODUCTIVE THOUGHTS. If

you follow sports, you are likely familiar with the process of coaches subbing in players during the game. If a player is playing poorly and it disrupts the flow of the game, coaches will often go to their bench to substitute a player into the game that may bring a fresh new approach. The hope is that it will instill an energy that sparks the team and allows them to compete at an elite level so they can win the game. This concept is very much the same when you are looking to retrain your brain to focus on the positive. Picture yourself as a coach as you assess your thoughts throughout your day. Any time that you acknowledge a negative thought that is counterproductive to what you are trying to achieve, go to your bench and make a substitution for

ARE MEANT TO DO ALL OUT AND MAKING YOUR MARK IS INEVITABLE. PURSUE THE THING YOU ARE MEANT TO DO a more productive thought. When you wake up 30 minutes early to do your morning routine and your brain defaults to its trained "it's too early," immediately sub out the thought with being excited to get up and pursue your dreams. It is a subtle shift, but it is one that can drastically change your attitude if you are diligent with your efforts.

RYB #3: SURROUND YOURSELF WITH POSITIVE PEOPLE. It is an extremely difficult process to flip the script to a positive outlook in a world that is full of cynicism and negativity. Not to sound like a pessimist, but if you are constantly surrounded by people with a negative attitude, then flipping the script may become insurmountable because your subconscious brain will consistently hear messages that reinforce your bad habits. The good news is that we have already touched on a skill set that you need to exercise in situations like this. While it may be challenging to do, it is essential that you cut back on time with negative people so you limit the exposure to unproductive thoughts. If a person's attitude is toxic enough, then you may need to eliminate them entirely from your life. This would certainly be the case if the person went out of their way to criticize your dreams and consistently took steps to stunt your progress. In this instance, be bold and eliminate them from your life. As you do this, be on the lookout for people that you can spend time with who model the positive attitude that you are trying to embrace. Be adamant about surrounding yourself with people who share your passions and will be contributors as you pursue your vision.

RYB #4: SURROUND YOURSELF WITH POSITIVE REINFORCEMENTS. The process of flipping the script is all about positive repetitions. Your mind can only consciously focus on one single thought at any given moment and it is important that you proactively fill these moments with the right kind of thoughts. Naturally, if you capitalize on these repetitions consistently enough, you will have no time for negative and you will eventually form positive habits that allow you to flip the script.

Building on the previous steps, another way you can capitalize here is by surrounding yourself with positive reinforcements. The ideal starting place is creating graphics that include your dreams, goals, and values so you can place them in locations where you see them strategically throughout your day. When a negative thought creeps in, you can use these lists to redirect your attention to more proactive thoughts about your future. It also makes sense to create a vision board that includes pictures, quotes, and words that capture your dreams effectively. Seeing this on a regular basis will keep your mind focused on the task at hand. No time for the negative.

RYB #5: REFLECT REGULARLY TO REINFORCE HABITS. One of the keys to living a successful life is learning to reflect regularly on your daily performance. When it comes to flipping the script, it is important that you find productive ways to redirect your thoughts to the positive when you fall short of expectations in your pursuit. The reality is that there will be times where you allow your mind to focus on the negative for extended periods of time. It is possible that you got lazy and did not "sub out" these thoughts effectively or you may have spent far too much time with a person who has a toxic negative presence. In either case, it is important that you reflect on your performance at the end of the day so you can acknowledge where you fell short. However, this is not where you want to spend your time. So, once you have acknowledged this, immediately focus on exactly what you will do to redirect to a positive approach the next day. It is important that you continue to repeat this process regularly so you can improve on your efforts consistently throughout your life.

RYB #6: MASTER THE ART OF MEDITATION. One of the ways to ensure that you keep a proactive mindset is by learning to control your emotions. There are hundreds of stimuli around us on a minute-by-minute basis and we must learn to respond to them the right way. It is critical to learn how to keep our mind calm so we are able to focus on the positive that will allow us to progress towards our vision. In *10 Secrets for Success and Inner Peace*, Dr. Wayne Dyer explains the importance of inner peace and taking the time to embrace silence: "When you're at peace, you radiate a different kind of energy than when you're stressed or depressed. The more peaceful you become, the easier you can deflect the negative energies of those you encounter." One way to achieve this is by taking the time to meditate on a regular basis. For the purposes of this book, we will keep things extremely simple. Find a quiet place where you can relax and sit in a comfortable position. Simply sit still, close your eyes, and breathe deeply in your nose and out your mouth in a controlled manner. As you do this, pay close attention to breathing and clear your mind. The key here is to simply acknowledge thoughts when they creep in your mind and allow them to pass. Eventually, you will develop the ability to keep a clear mind and you will gain control over your emotions. This simple exercise will allow you to maintain a calm and focused mindset throughout your day regardless of your circumstances.

> " The more peaceful you become, the easier you can deflect the negative energies of those you encounter.
> -@DrWayneWDyer

RYB #7: INVEST IN PROACTIVE SUPPORT STRUCTURE. Each of the previous steps is about putting a structure in place around you that will maximize exposure to positive thoughts. Building on these initiatives, you can increase your chances of flipping the script by investing in a growth system that keeps your mind focused sharply on proactive thoughts that allow you to progress towards your vision. The morning routine is one of the most effective ways to make sure you are setting the tone in your day for opportunities to achieve your goals and dreams. By starting with a simple structure that includes reading the right books, journaling and revisiting goals, you can train your mind to focus on the exact thoughts that you have chosen. This is an essential progression because it gets your mind in a proactive place to fend off negative stimuli that are commonly present around you. Combine this with simple gratitude activities and you will be on your way to flipping the script on negative thoughts.

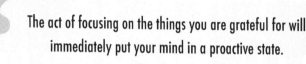

> The act of focusing on the things you are grateful for will immediately put your mind in a proactive state.
> -@coytecooper

The Gift That Is Gratitude

There are few things that are more effective at eliminating negative thoughts than learning to cultivate an attitude of gratitude. Because your mind is only capable of holding one conscious thought at any given moment, the simple act of focusing on the things that you are grateful for will immediately put your mind in a proactive state. When you are grateful, you have no time for negative thoughts that are counterproductive to progressing towards your vision. Gratitude is a gift because it teaches you to be happy with your current situation in life. Regardless of who you are or what your current situation in life is, there are always opportunities to find things that you are grateful for around you. The ability to capitalize on this process is a skill set that can completely transform your life. When your mind is in a state of gratitude, you will attract people and opportunities that would not have previously been available to you. The outstanding thing is that the actual state of being grateful is something that anyone can capture by investing in simple daily action items that we will discuss in this chapter. This is something we teach participants to do within their normal daily routine in the Impressions 28-Day Growth Challenge and it helps drastically transform people's lives in a short amount of time. Here are some of the basic action items you can take to capitalize on an attitude of gratitude.

CREATE A GRATITUDE LIST: The key to gratitude and growth in general is keeping things simple. This activity epitomizes the concept of simplicity, as it is something that anybody can easily embrace at any point in his or her life. All you need from a resource standpoint is a pen and a piece of paper to do it (or a computer if you prefer it). Beyond this, it is simply about carving out 5-10 minutes in your daily schedule to write down all of the things that you are grateful for in your life. The most challenging thing to overcome when doing this activity is the initial starting point. Whenever I work with people on creating a gratitude list, they tend to think that the items need to be major, life altering things that can be difficult to come by. It is important to recognize that there are all kinds of gifts around us each day that we often take for granted. Some examples include our families, health, ability to provide, and simply being alive. There are all kinds of people around us who have these things taken from them and we need to be grateful for the fact that we still have them in our lives. Write as many of these down as you can possibly think of and then place the list in a location where you will see it each day. The ideal time to see this is in the morning with your growth routine so you start your day with a sense of gratitude. However, there is never a bad time to see your gratitude list and you can use it as a resource to immediately redirect negative thoughts when you have them.

SEND LETTERS OF APPRECIATION: One of the keys to flipping the script on negative thoughts is learning to get your mind to regularly focus on the positive in the people around you. In addition to cultivating more productive relationships, the act of writing gratitude letters also gets your mind into a state of abundance that naturally lends itself to positive thinking. Rather than focusing on the negative, this activity teaches you to narrow in on attributes that are good so you can express your gratitude in a meaningful manner to someone who has had a positive impact on your life. The key here is authenticity because the exercise will not work if you do not believe that the person deserves to receive the email or letter. To get started here, create a list of five people who have done something to make your life better and then commit to writing letters to them over the next week. You will be amazed at how this simple act of showing your appreciation for someone cultivates an abundance mindset. Even better is that some of them will likely respond and you will be inspired by the impact you were able to make in a simple, 5-10 minute exercise. For some, it will be impactful enough that you commit to making it a regular part of your weekly routine.

INVEST IN A "GRATITUDE BANK": We are going to stick with the theme of simplicity for this third initiative. This means that there are no excuses for not making them happen. They are easy to implement, but you must have the discipline to follow through when there are distractions around you. For this activity, you simply need a jar, box, or container where you can make daily gratitude deposits on sheets of paper. At the end of your day, place a date on the sheet of paper and write down one good thing that happened to you during the day. Do this for one full month and then pull out all of the sheets of paper to read the things you have to be grateful for. You will be astonished at all the gifts you have that you normally take for granted. This will be a valuable reminder that you need to keep a proactive mindset so that you are constantly aware of the gifts around you that often go unnoticed.

COMMIT RANDOM ACTS OF KINDNESS: The final gratitude activity that you can invest in is random acts of kindness. It is likely that most of you have heard this term and many of you have actually been involved in random acts that are designed to make other people's lives better. The complexity of these acts vary as they can be as simple as holding a door for someone or as complex as finding a way to create a scholarship fund to honor someone's life. However, the important thing here is not that you try to do something major. While this is great if you have the opportunity to do something more complex, the key in this initiative is for you to learn to start doing nice things for other people. Similar to the previous steps, it will put your mind in a state of abundance that will drastically transform all areas of your life.

Don't Confuse Simplicity With Lack of Impact

One of the mistakes that people commonly make when it comes to personal development and success is they believe that simple activities are not enough to take their life to another level. This is a misperception because meaningful accomplishments and lives are almost always founded on simple fundamentals that successful individuals practice on a daily basis over extended periods of time. Most of the initiatives outlined in this chapter are very simple to apply in your life. However, it is important that you do not confuse this with being easy because complacency is the status quo in our society. While they are simple to implement, they are also easy to pass up on because of the clutter that is often present in our life. It is essential that you cultivate an ability to narrow in on key initiatives because they have the potential to drastically transform your life by allowing you to flip the script on negative thoughts.

Simple Lifestyle Changes

Beyond the previous initiatives designed to crowd out negative thoughts, there are also some lifestyle changes that you can make to increase your chances of maximizing exposure to positive thoughts. Rather than seeing them as separate initiatives, consider them as additional elements that can be a part of an overall attack to eliminate all of your negative thoughts. While these are different than the previous initiatives, they will reinforce flipping the script and will keep your mind focused on proactive thoughts that will allow you to progress towards your dreams. Each will make an impact on your life if you have the self-discipline to make them a daily part of your routine.

EXERCISE. Research has shown that exercise is one of the best ways to get your mind in a proactive state. While the initial commitment can be challenging, the process has both physiological and mental benefits that can drastically improve the quality of life for people who have the self-discipline to make being active a part of their routine. Movement is a natural part of being human and doing 20-30 minutes of exercise each day allows you to capitalize on these benefits. In addition to improving your health, the process of getting workouts in each day builds confidence because you are following through on an activity that you know is important to your life. Studies have shown that exercise makes you far more productive because it reduces stress levels and improves your body's ability to handle challenging tasks throughout your day. The end result is a more positive approach that increases your chances of flipping the script on unproductive thoughts.

WATCH LESS TELEVISION. As we have mentioned previously, the average American watches at least three hours of television each day. Remember the 1,095 hours annually that we previously mentioned? Much of this time is spent on programs that are littered with negative thoughts. While I am certainly not telling you to give up all of your favorite television shows, you may want to consider the impact that watching these programs have on your mindset. Pay attention the next time you watch them and be cognizant of the types of messages that they include. In addition, take note of the impact that they have on your attitude while watching them. Beyond just the time you spend watching the programs, the negative dialogue after the show often extends to conversations with friends in person and followers on social media. The key here is to assess this habit and determine whether it is a productive way to progress towards your vision. If the answer is "no," then you should consider reducing your time spent watching television and reallocate it to something that is far more productive.

FIND SOMETHING TO LOOK FORWARD TO. In your progression, there will be times where you feel down and question your ability to achieve your vision. This is a natural tendency as a human. This is especially true as you work to establish the right habits in your life. However, there are strategies outlined in this chapter that are designed to help you avoid the frequency of these moments. By focusing sharply on gratitude and the positive, you can decrease the chances of feelings that you would prefer to not have. I am not saying that it will be easy, but it is absolutely possible if you strengthen your mind's ability to focus on productive thoughts. Another strategy to help avoid these thoughts is to always have something in your life that you are looking forward to in the future.

FIND WAYS TO UTILIZE YOUR STRENGTHS. There are few things that will make you feel better than when you get to work in your strength zone. Have you ever personally had the opportunity to be involved in activities where you were able to perform at a really high level? One where you were able to shine and do things that other people around you weren't able to do? If so, then you know what I am talking about here. There is something really uplifting about being able to use your areas of genius in a practical situation. With this being the case, it makes sense to be proactive about finding ways to operate in your strength zones often so you can replicate these feelings on a regular basis. When this is done strategically on initiatives that allow you to progress towards your vision, the positive feelings will compound because you will be taking steps to fulfill your purpose. This will also allow you to naturally find more challenging situations that are conducive to growing and extending your skill sets. The development, combined with the use of your areas of genius, will allow your confidence to soar because you will be doing exactly what you are meant to be doing.

> There are few things that will make you feel better than when you get to work in your strength zone.
>
> -@coytecooper

THE IMPACT OF ATTITUDE ON OTHERS

If you want to be successful, then you must learn to focus on the positive so that your daily efforts are productive and allow you to progress efficiently towards your aspirations. Given that negativity is so prevalent, you have an opportunity to be a "game changer" in a variety of different environments (e.g., home, team, work) if you are proactive in how you approach situations. However, as explained by Amber Olson Rourke, Chief Marketing Officer for Nerium International, consistency in our approach is essential to make this happen: "If our moods go up and down and our actions are inconsistent, if we smile at people sometimes and walk past them stony-faced at others because we're 'having a bad day,' then our positive and negative impact may just cancel each other out, and the net effect may not add up to much. Worse, if we more consistently lean to the negative - always complaining, typically looking at the problems rather than the solutions, playing the role of critic and cynic - then we may be having a net negative ripple effect, bringing the world down." Similar to what we talked about in the introduction, you have an opportunity to have a butterfly effect on the world, but keep in mind that this can be either negative or positive depending on your approach. Consistency in flipping the script will put you in a position to make your mark on the world in a meaningful way. It all starts with your ability to create a mindset where you are focused on being a part of the solution.

> Consistency in flipping the script on negative thoughts will put you in a position to make your mark on the world.
> -@coytecooper

DON'T COMPLICATE THE PROCESS

When it comes to your attitude or progress in general, your success is going to depend on your ability to simplify your daily approach. There were a variety of different strategies that were presented in this chapter that will help you to flip the script on negative thoughts in your life. It is not realistic to think that you will implement them all in a short period of time. This is particularly true if you are in the process of implementing other concepts presented in earlier chapters in the book. The key to your success is going to be in your progression to add productive initiatives to your life on a regular basis. For now, focus on implementing one or two initiatives this week and track your progress. An ideal starting point is to track your negative thoughts so you gain an awareness of the regularity of unproductive responses in your environment. Following this activity, you will likely be more motivated to implement other simple steps that are designed to crowd out negative thoughts. If you continue to grow and progress in the different initiatives outlined in the chapter, you will eventually get to the point where you are one of the few who are successful in flipping the script on negative thoughts.

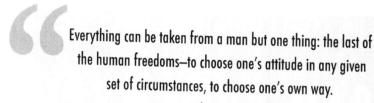

> Everything can be taken from a man but one thing: the last of the human freedoms—to choose one's attitude in any given set of circumstances, to choose one's own way.
> - Viktor Frankl

THE LAST OF HUMAN FREEDOMS

It is important that you acknowledge that your attitude is always something that is under your control. While you may not believe it now, you always choose the thoughts that you have on a consistent basis. This is something that no one can take from you regardless of the circumstances you are facing. If you don't believe me, then hear it from someone who faced extremely dire circumstances and still chose to focus on the positive. Viktor Frankl, concentration camp survivor and author of *Man's Search for Meaning*, explained this about the power of choice: "Everything can be taken from a man but one thing: the last of the human freedoms—to choose one's attitude in any given set of circumstances, to choose one's own way." The key to flipping the script is to not allow external circumstances to control your attitude. The weather is never the reason why you have a bad attitude. Nor are other people's actions, a lack of sleep, your dog's counterproductive habits, other people's driving abilities, or a slew of other things we encounter each day. With each situation that you face, you always have a choice of what they mean to you. While your circumstances will certainly not always be ideal, you have the power to choose to focus on the positive in each situation so you are able to make your response productive. The key is to regularly exercise your right to choose the thoughts that will allow you to earn the right to live your dreams.

THE MAKE YOUR MARK MASTER

ANNE FRANK

It is extremely rare to find an individual who has such an extraordinary mindset that they make a lasting impression on the world. Yet this is exactly what Anne Frank was able to accomplish in her short life. Born in 1929, Frank and her family were forced to flee from the Nazis and go into hiding for two years during World War II. Despite facing dire circumstances, Anne kept her spirits up as she wrote in a diary each day to reflect on her situation throughout the war. Her entries demonstrated thoughts and feelings that were far beyond her teenage years. After being sent to a concentration camp, she came down with typhus in the spring of 1945 and died. Her dad Otto, who had been separated from Anne and her sister, found her journal and was blown away by the depth of her entries. He pushed hard to have the work published and was successful on June 25, 1947. The book, entitled *The Diary of a Young Girl*, was so powerful that it has since been published in 67 different languages. Her story is one that illustrates the power of the human spirit and has inspired people to find the positive in their situation. As a result, young Anne Frank and her optimistic approach have made a lasting impact on the world.

KEY SUMMARY POINTS

O   Attitude is always your choice. Regardless of your circumstances, you can choose to focus on the positive so that you have a proactive mindset that seeks out opportunities to progress towards your vision. You should never allow external circumstances to control your thoughts and attitude.

O   Studies have shown that up to 80 percent of our thoughts in a day are negative. With an average of 48.6 thoughts per minute, this is the equivalent of having a negative thought approximately every two seconds. While these are often unconscious, they still take up precious time that could have been used on progressing towards our aspirations.

O   Negative thoughts have been shown to trigger the human response system and result in unfavorable health and performance consequences. On the flip side, studies have also shown that cultivating a more positive attitude can result in a variety of benefits that are essential to success. Among them are being more creative and solving problems in a more efficient manner.

O   The key to flipping the script is focusing on creating a structure that crowds out the negative. The Retrain Your Brain (RYB) and gratitude exercises are simple strategies that will teach your mind to focus on the positive so that you can regularly progress towards your vision.

CHAPTER 10

No Permission Needed to Pursue Your Dreams

> *Criticism comes to those who stand out.*
> - Seth Godin

WHEN YOU ARE a big dreamer, criticism comes with the territory. Period. There are a couple primary reasons why this is the case. First, you are embarking on a journey where you are willing to take more risks than others and this alone gives you more repetitions that people can and will critique. Given that it is common to criticize in our society, you can expect that your active approach will put you in a position to receive more feedback, whether it is something you seek out or not. Second, the moment you set lofty aspirations that are "unreasonable" by normal standards, you will immediately attract negative attention because your expectations will make people uncomfortable who are living within their comfort zone. Your approach to realize full potential will make others uneasy and their criticism will reflect the fact that they need to justify their current effort level. In these instances, it is not your job to adjust your standards to make them feel better. It is not your fault that they have chosen a lifestyle where they avoid risks so they can maintain the status quo. The good news here is that you do not need their permission to pursue your dreams. It is always within your power to focus sharply on things under your control so you can progress towards your vision. The tricky part is that not all criticism should be ignored and avoided. While we will spend a majority of the chapter touching on this negative type of criticism, it is important to recognize the role that constructive criticism has on growth and realizing our full potential. We must be willing to acknowledge areas where we can improve our efforts if we are going to live our dreams and make our mark on the world.

The Good Kind Of Criticism

It would be a mistake if the message in this chapter were that all forms of criticism were destructive and should be ignored. This would reinforce the fixed mind mentality because we would be assuming that we are always correct and there is no room for improvement. The truth is that criticism can be a major asset to your growth when it comes from people who are knowledgeable and who are giving it to you for the right reasons. So, how do you know if someone is providing it in a productive manner? While this is a tricky thing to know, the key lies in the reason why they are providing you the feedback. If they are only criticizing you to provide feedback to improve, then it would be considered constructive and you should at least consider their advice. After all, there are great people who will offer you insights that will be essential to you realizing your full potential. Former legendary Great Britain Prime Minister Winston Churchill had this to say about this form of feedback: "Criticism may not be agreeable, but it is necessary. It fulfills the same function as pain in the human body. It calls attention to an unhealthy state of things." When your performance levels are not up to par or you are making decisions that are less than ideal, it is important that you keep an open mind about criticism so you can improve your efforts and move towards full potential.

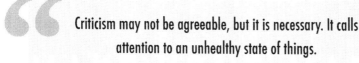

> Criticism may not be agreeable, but it is necessary. It calls attention to an unhealthy state of things.
> - Winston Churchill

ALWAYS KEEP YOUR MIND OPEN FOR IMPROVEMENTS

When criticism comes your way, the key is to strive to never take it personally no matter whom it comes from. This is even the case if the feedback is not constructive. In the times where criticism comes, your first reaction will often be to resist the information because receiving negative comments is not fun. If you are going to reach your full potential, you must fight off this urge so you can embrace a growth mindset where you are looking for ways to improve. For this to happen, you should always immediately scan the information to see if there is anything you can learn from it. In many instances, you will be able to find something that will allow you to enhance your efforts. In the times where the criticism is not warranted and/or productive, the one thing you may learn is how not to treat others. This is still an opportunity to grow and you should keep this in mind as you interact with others. There will be times where you should heed this advice from the great Major League Baseball player Willie Mays: "In order to excel, you must be completely dedicated to your chosen sport. You must also be prepared to work hard and be willing to accept constructive criticism. Without one-hundred percent dedication, you won't be able to do this." While you may not be playing a sport, the key is to take constructive criticism and turn it into something that will allow you to progress towards your dreams. Actress Halle Berry added this about processing criticism and using it in a productive manner: "When I was a kid, my mother told me that if you can't be a good loser, you can't be a good winner. If you can't take criticism, then you don't deserve the praise." This is excellent advice that refers to the ability to open your mind up to improving through feedback. It also indicates that there will be times when you need to deal with destructive criticism that can threaten your ability to realize your vision.

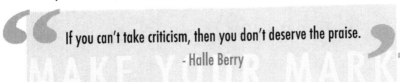

"If you can't take criticism, then you don't deserve the praise.
- Halle Berry"

NOT ALL CRITICISM IS PRODUCTIVE

When you really break things down, there will be times when you get criticism that is not worth your time. This will often be the case when someone is jealous of your efforts and they are critical of you because it reflects better on them. In the times when you assess and determine that the feedback is not constructive, it is important to move on from it immediately and focus your brain on things that will allow you to proactively move towards your vision. It is impossible for you to please everyone so you must be ready to block out negative criticism when it is not justified and/or productive. In these instances, you can cultivate a mindset where you learn to embrace the fact that it is a good thing that you are being criticized.

After all, it tells you that you have set lofty aspirations that make other people uncomfortable. It also presents an opportunity for you to develop thicker skin as you gain momentum in your pursuit to live your dreams. In the times where you continue to struggle with this concept, revisit this quote by Zig Ziglar and remind yourself that not all people's intentions are good: "Don't be distracted by criticism. Remember, the only taste of success some people have is when they take a bite out of you."

Only Way To Avoid Criticism

The misperception that people commonly have when pursuing success is the belief that they should be able to develop a flawless approach that is void of criticism. This is not realistic because your lofty aspirations will make it inevitable that people will criticize you because your standards will make them uncomfortable. In the words of Aristotle, "there is only one way to avoid criticism: do nothing, say nothing, and be nothing." Because none of these things are an option for big dreamers, you must learn to embrace criticism as part of the process. In fact, you can even shift your mindset to see it as a good thing because this means that you have likely chosen dreams that are challenging enough to demand your full potential. One of the greatest American authors of all-time Francis Scott Fitzgerald provided this optimistic approach to processing negative feedback: "I've always looked on criticism as a sort of envious tribute." When you have people paying attention to what you are doing and critiquing your work, see it as a good thing because you are likely doing something well enough to warrant their attention. The important thing is to process it in a productive manner and to focus on doing what is right based on your vision and passions.

> There is only one way to avoid criticism:
> do nothing, say nothing, and be nothing.
> - Aristotle

Always Do What's Right

When it comes to pursuing your vision, you job is not to do what is popular. It is to do what is right. Never make it your objective to settle for the status quo. Instead, set lofty aspirations and take the often-unpopular path that is necessary to make it a reality. Napoleon

Hill, author of *Think and Grow Rich*, had this to say about choosing your own path: "If the thing you wish to do is right, and you believe in it, go ahead and do it! Put your dream across, and never mind what 'they' say if you meet with temporary defeat, for 'they,' perhaps, do not know that every failure brings with it the seed of an equivalent success." In the times where you are criticized for your pursuit, it is important that you remind yourself that you are doing what is necessary to live out your purpose. Because you are pursuing lofty aspirations, negative feedback is inevitable. When times like these come and you are doubting yourself, remind yourself of this feedback from Eleanor Roosevelt: "Do what you feel in your heart to be right - for you'll be criticized anyway. You'll be damned if you do. And damned if you don't." Considering you will likely be criticized regardless, you might as well take the path where you pursue your purpose and full potential. It is the route that will be most likely to lead you to success and happiness.

You Don't Need Anyone's Permission

If you follow the steps outlined in this book there will come a time where your vision is clear and you will be excited to get out and make remarkable things happen in your life. You acknowledge that it is going to take a tremendous amount of work, but you are energized by the thought of earning the right to live your dreams. However, this can quickly change as you get out and take action if your mind is not right. As you start to announce your intentions to the world, it is fairly certain that you will be met with resistance that you must push through. This often comes in the form of negative feedback from others who question your aspirations and your ability to achieve them.   The mistake that people commonly make is they take this personally and they allow it to impact them mentally. This small amount of friction can cause people to doubt their dreams and their ability to make them a reality. If you have progressed to this point, you have allowed their opinions to progress too far and you should never allow this to happen in the future. Let's get one thing straight right now. You don't need anyone's permission to pursue your dreams. People are always going to be entitled to their opinion and they will often voice this when they disagree with your approach. Regardless of the circumstances, the most productive response when pursuing your dreams is to never take negative comments personally. While people have the right to voice their opinions, they are simply that and you can always choose to ignore them and move on. There is no need to dwell on negativity because there is really only one person's opinion that matters when it comes to the pursuit of your dreams.

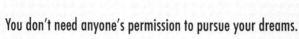

You don't need anyone's permission to pursue your dreams.
-@coytecooper

THE ONLY OPINION THAT MATTERS

There is one opinion that truly matters when pursuing your dreams and that is your own. It does not make a difference what other people think about your aspirations if you believe in them enough to pursue them and strive to make them a reality. However, this is a lot more challenging than it sounds because fending off criticism can be a difficult task. The good news is that you have all the tools necessary in this book to develop supreme confidence in your vision and ability to bring it to fruition. The key is investing in a daily process that reinforces your positive attitude and that allows you to stay in touch with your aspirations. When you are connected to a crystal clear vision, it will provide the clarity necessary to fend off the negative criticism that will come your way. Constantly make investments to progress towards your vision so you build the momentum necessary to make it a reality.

Your opinion is the one that will truly matter as you strive to live your dreams. Believing alone will not guarantee your accomplishments, but it will give you the best chance possible of bringing them to fruition. You must first convince yourself that you are deserving of this honor by proving you are ready to earn the right to live your dreams. No short cuts, remember?

THE ONES WHO MATTER MOST

When it comes to the pursuit of your dreams, it is important that we clarify something before moving ahead. While you don't need anyone's permission to pursue them, you should always consider and include the most important people in your life when determining your exact path. This is the primary reason why family and close friends were not included in the previous section. They should simply always be a part of your decision-making process. The opinions of people who are a top priority in your life should always come into play as you make decisions about your future. If your partner has concerns about your dreams and voices them, the last thing you should do is blow them off if the relationship is important to you. This is also true when it comes to people closest to you (e.g., parents, siblings) that care about your future and well-being. Because they normally have your best interests in mind, you can expect to get constructive criticism that should influence your decisions. Your aspirations should never come at a cost to neglecting people who are truly important to you. If you do make this decision, then the criticism that comes would be warranted and you should strongly consider it. Instead, your dreams, when chosen properly, should allow you to enhance these people's lives in some unique way on a regular basis. It is the destructive criticism outside of your close circle that you need to be aware of and ready to deflect as you pursue your vision with your full attention.

> Your aspirations should never come at a cost to neglecting people who are truly important to you.
>
> -@coytecooper

KEYS TO SHUNNING CRITICISM

It is important that you learn to shun destructive criticism. It is inevitable that it will come and you must learn to brush it off so you don't allow it to slow up your momentum. If you are at a stage in your progression where this task is difficult for you, it is important that you focus on taking daily steps to build your confidence levels. Remember that your success depends on consistent repetition and the ability to focus on strategic initiatives that strengthen your mindset. When you have a structure in place that is designed to advance you towards your vision, it is far easier to brush off criticism because you will have confidence in the way you are living your life. It will not matter what other people think because your decisions will be connected to your purpose and the path to pursuing your dreams. This process can take time so be patient as you develop the clarity and confidence necessary to truly shun criticism. In the meantime, simply invest in the following initiatives so you can stay well connected to your vision.

1. **REVISIT VISION OVER AND OVER.** We have mentioned this step multiple times in this book. Rather than see it as redundancy, call it a repetition that is necessary to emphasize the importance of the concept. When it comes to realizing your full potential, there are few things more important than being clear as to what you would like to achieve in your life. Once you know your vision, the way to ensure this happens is by revisiting your vision on a daily basis. The same could be said about your goals and values. Every time you revisit them, it is a repetition in strengthening your confidence in your ability to achieve them. So how

does this relate to criticism? My guess is you already know the answer. When you build confidence in your long-term aspirations, you diminish the need to have anyone's permission to pursue them. In addition, your clarity will allow you to quickly brush off criticism because you will be locked in on the exact life you plan to live. The more frequent the repetitions, the more likely you will be able to shun negative feedback so you can spend your time on productive thoughts and initiatives.

2. PRACTICE POSITIVE REPETITIONS. The process of revisiting your vision is the first step you should take when investing in quality positive repetitions. Focusing on your end destination sharpens your clarity and allows you to progress with a meaningful approach. However, it is not the only step you can take to strengthen your ability to shun criticism. There are examples littered throughout this book that are designed to help you progress towards your goals and dreams. In each instance, these are opportunities that improve your confidence in your ability to achieve great things. If your dream is to become a best selling author, then it is essential that you do something about it every single day to make it a reality. As you start to believe in your ability to accomplish this aspiration, then criticism will start to matter less and less to you. It is as if you are taking steps away from all the negative noise (criticism) each time you make an investment. Eventually you will move so far away that you will no longer hear it. The key is to continually invest so you eventually have the confidence required to shun criticism.

3. EMBRACE STRUCTURE OF SUPPORT SYSTEM. There will be times that criticism will be difficult to handle. This is the case no matter who you are. Nobody is immune to feeling the sting of criticism and reacting to it at some point in their life. This is when it is so important that you have people around you that are supportive of your dreams. When you have quality people surrounding you who care deeply about you, they will help pick you up in the times where you are struggling with criticism. Big dreams require that you have people who believe in you and what you are trying to achieve because they will keep you focused in times where you face adversity. Be sure that you take the time to find these people and make them aware of your vision so they can support you as you strive to make your mark on the world.

4. PRACTICING PERSISTENCE. There are going to be few things more important than learning to practice persistence when it comes to pursuing your dreams. It is inevitable that you will fall short of expectations when you set big dreams that require that you live way outside of your comfort zone. When you face adversity in your journey, it is a necessity that you stay focused sharply on the end destination and what it will take to make your vision a reality. In short, you must be remarkably persistent in your approach. Fail to follow through on your daily growth repetitions? Don't make it a big deal. Instead, assess why you fell short and commit to getting back on track immediately. Be as efficient as possible in your pursuit to focus on productive steps to live your dreams. Fall short on achieving a goal that you invested heavily in during the past year? While you initially will not enjoy this result, it is important that you embrace it as an opportunity to grow and immediately find ways to improve so it doesn't happen again the next time. Receive stinging criticism about your lack of ability to achieve your goals? Continually remind yourself not to take it personally and instead see it as a sign that you are on the right track because people are paying attention to what you are doing. The point is that you will need to be extremely persistent in your pursuit to make your vision a reality. Big dreams are not meant for people who are going to give up at the first sign of adversity.

5. REJECT NOTION OF "NO'S" BEING PERMANENT. It is guaranteed that you will receive "no's" in the pursuit to live your dreams. In fact, you should probably get used to the fact that you will get far more

228 COYTE COOPER, PH.D.

of these responses when you have lofty ambitions. If your dreams matter enough to you, then you need to learn to reject the notion of "no's" being permanent when you face them. They are nothing more than small speed bumps on the road to your end destination. In the times where you face larger amounts of these responses and you start to doubt yourself, remind yourself of the amazing people that have battled through adversity and rejected "no's" as being permanent on the way to amazing things. You too can become a part of this group of high performers who made their mark on the world.

- Oprah Winfrey was fired from her first job as an anchor in Baltimore because they believed she was not a good fit for television. She rejected this opinion and went on to become one of the top television personalities in the world. Oprah is now a billionaire who impacts millions of people's lives on a daily basis.

- Sir James Dyson fell short of expectations 5,126 times before he found a vacuum cleaner prototype that worked. His persistence paid off as Dyson has become the top selling bagless vacuum cleaner brand in the United States. Sir James Dyson is also now a billionaire.

- Vera Wang failed to make the U.S. Olympic figure-skating team before going on to become an editor at Vogue. She was passed over for the editor-in-chief position, but did not let this deter her as she instead decided to start designing wedding gowns at the age of 40. Today she is one of the premier designers in the fashion industry and runs a business worth over $1 billion.

The Bigger The Dream...

There is a general law that always seems to be true when it

comes to vision. The bigger your dream, the more criticism you can expect as you embark on your journey. This is absolutely the case as you realize success because big time dreams tend to make people who have settled for the status quo uncomfortable. As you progress towards your dreams, this generally comes with more attention and this opens you up to additional people who will sometimes have an opinion on how you are choosing to live your life. The good news here is that when you choose a noble vision, this will also come with positive comments from people who believe in your approach. If you do a solid job creating energy around your vision, this will result in attracting quality people who want to jump on board to help you achieve your dreams. In the process, you must be able to wade through the negative comments that come with big dreams. The most impactful leaders of all-time are individuals who learned to deal with the negative attention that comes with living an extraordinary life.

THE ALL-TIME GREATS & CRITICISM

All of the greatest leaders that this world has ever seen faced tremendous amounts of criticism in their pursuit to make their mark on the world. In fact, their lofty aspirations ensured that they had significantly more negative attention than the average person. The differentiating factor for these individuals is that they determined early on that they did not need other people's permission to pursue their dreams. Abraham Lincoln did not need the approval from an entire country to do what he believed was right while carrying out his purpose. The same can be said of Nelson Mandela and Mahatma Gandhi. Each of them had crystal clear visions that inspired them to take productive action regardless of the criticism they received. No amount of adversity was going to stop them from pursuing the thing they believed they were put on this earth to accomplish.

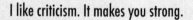

> ## I like criticism. It makes you strong.
> - KingJames

USE CRITICISM AS MOTIVATION

Many of the most successful people in their fields choose to take a different route when dealing with criticism. In effect, they learn to reframe negative feedback into something that fuels them to higher performance levels. Rather than taking it personally, they become highly efficient at using it as motivation. Four-time National Basketball Association (NBA) Most Valuable Player and business mogul Lebron James explained that he actually likes criticism because it has helped shape him into a stronger player and person. Not personal. Inspiration to fuel his efforts towards an end destination. You see the distinction? By reframing the situation, they use these doubts as a tool to perform at a higher level because they are driven by the opportunity to prove other people wrong. While the central focus should always be on realizing your full potential, there is nothing wrong with being driven by other people's opinions as long as this is done in a productive manner. In the words of early 1900's motion picture star Will Rogers, "Acknowledge criticism, but not subdued by it. Keep it within as a constant reminder, to provoke you enough to fight and disprove it."

> ## First they ignore you. Then they laugh at you.
> ## Then they fight you. Then you win.
> - Mahatma Gandhi

IGNORE. LAUGH. FIGHT. WIN.

The legendary leader Mahatma Gandhi has a quote that sums up his extraordinary path to achieve his dreams: "First they ignore you.

Then they laugh at you. Then they fight you. Then you win." This was something he lived daily as he strived for equality in his home country of India. He faced extreme adversity and criticism in his journey. Yet he did not allow this to take him away from what he believed was his purpose. When Gandhi started his pursuit, he was first ignored because his efforts were not noticeable on a large scale. He was like the butterfly in this sense. However, because he was truly passionate about his cause and had a clear vision, he built momentum to the point where people noticed him and laughed at his efforts. This was the part where people recognized his dreams and criticized him because it made them uncomfortable. This did not bother him though because his vision was crystal clear and he continued to pursue his passion with more energy. Once he had done enough to truly make a difference through his efforts and challenged the status quo, people fought him because it threatened their normal way of living. Yet Gandhi chose not to fight back with physical violence and instead inspired millions of people to follow him because of his contagious passion. Eventually, he earned the right to live his dreams and he won. Remember "The Butterfly Effect" from earlier in the book? Gandhi was a single person that made a remarkable influence on the world because of his ability to shun criticism so he could continue to pursue his vision.

NELSON MANDELA

Nelson Mandela was an extraordinary leader who left a lasting impression on the world that will always be remembered. This was apparent on December 5, 2013 when the world mourned his loss following his death in Johannesburg, South Africa. However, this worldwide respect and legendary status was far from being a reality throughout his life. Fighting for the end of a racially divided system in South Africa, he faced extreme adversity in his life in the form of discrimination and violence. In fact, throughout the course of his life, he spent 27 years in prison to fight for the vision that he believed to be his purpose. While most people would allow this time in prison to break them or leave them seeking revenge, he used the adversity to fuel his efforts and eventually succeeded in his valiant efforts. On top of achieving racial equality, he went on to become the President of his country at the age of 75 in 1994. He served in this role until 1999 and was a highly respected world leader throughout the rest of his life. Following his death, he continues to make his mark on the world because of his inspirational efforts during his time on Earth.

KEY SUMMARY POINTS

O   When you set lofty goals, criticism is inevitable. Rather than try to avoid it, embrace it as an opportunity to fuel your efforts. The most successful people use negative feedback to identify ways to grow and to motivate them to achieve at a much higher level.

O   One of the keys to fending off criticism is to know your vision, goals, and values, and then to strive to always do what is right no matter what the circumstances are surrounding you. When your vision is crystal clear, it will allow you to brush off criticism because you will feel confident in the way that you have chosen to live your life.

O   Given that criticism is so prominent, one of the keys to success in the pursuit of your aspirations is being proactive about focusing on opportunities to progress. Revisiting vision, practicing positive reps, embracing a support system, and being proactively persistent are all ways to ensure that you are able to shun criticism.

O   You do not need anyone's permission to pursue your dreams. When you receive criticism, always remind yourself that it has no bearing on your ability to progress unless you allow it to negatively influence your mindset.

S INEVITABLE. PURSUE THE THING YOU ARE MEANT TO DO ALL OUT AND MAKING YOUR MARK IS INEVITABLE. PUR

CHAPTER 11

CREATE A HIGH PERFORMANCE LIFESTYLE

Make each day your masterpiece.
- John Wooden

IF YOU WANT to change your life, then you must be willing to change your habits. It is really that simple. The legendary leadership expert Dr. John Maxwell explained this about habits: "You'll never change your life until you change something you do daily. The secret of your success is found in your daily routine." It is exactly what is included in this routine that is the differentiating factor for highly successful people. You see, individuals such as Dr. Maxwell have strategically chosen daily high performance behaviors that allow them to rapidly progress towards their goals and dreams. But choosing, as you know, is only one part of the equation. High performers also put a structure in place that allows them to consistently act on desired behaviors until they are able to eventually make them productive habits. By now, you already know that this is a lot more challenging than it sounds. Life always presents clutter that you must cut through if you are going to ensure that your daily actions are in direct alignment with your aspirations. The good news is that you have been building your skill sets throughout the book and are now ready for this exact challenge. The key is to be aware of the exact obstacles you will be facing so you can create a high performance lifestyle that will lead you to your full potential and the opportunity to achieve all of your dreams.

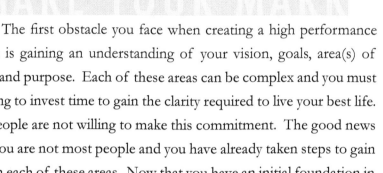

The secret of your success is found in your daily routine.
-@JohnCMaxwell

The first obstacle you face when creating a high performance lifestyle is gaining an understanding of your vision, goals, area(s) of genius, and purpose. Each of these areas can be complex and you must be willing to invest time to gain the clarity required to live your best life. Most people are not willing to make this commitment. The good news is that you are not most people and you have already taken steps to gain clarity in each of these areas. Now that you have an initial foundation in place, the challenge becomes sitting down and connecting these long-term aspirations and skill sets to daily initiatives that will allow you to make your mark on the world. This takes some serious self-discipline, and again, most people are not willing to invest the energy necessary to know exactly what they need to do each day to progress towards their goals, and eventually, dreams.

Finally, even when we connect our daily intentions with long-term aspirations, there are still so many distractions around us that demand our attention and urge us to settle for the easiest path. This chapter is designed to help you overcome these obstacles by showing you how to create a high performance calendar that will allow you to establish world-class habits. With some structure and disciplined follow through, you will be on your way to living your absolute best life.

What Is a High Performance Lifestyle?

The goal of this chapter is to provide you with foundational information to help you cultivate a high performance lifestyle. Given that this is the case, it makes sense to first start by defining this concept and explaining how it can drastically impact your life. In sports, peak performance is a common term that describes situations where athletes perform at their highest level and "peak" during competition. This phenomenon includes instances where an athlete gets into the zone and things tend to come more instinctively to them. This was something I experienced personally in high school when I won a National Championship and was honored with the Outstanding Wrestler Award of the entire tournament. I was fortunate to have a world-class coach at the time and he prepared me so well that I competed to my absolute full potential at the event. As I reflect on this experience, there is no question that lifestyle played a role in me peaking and getting the chance to realize my goal.

Interestingly, while common in the sports arena, this is not a concept that has been widely applied to other normal living situations. It absolutely should though. For the purposes of this book, the high performance lifestyle encompasses you striving to create a daily set of behaviors that will allow you to live to full potential. In essence, these are daily behaviors that, when performed consistently, will help you to establish world-class habits. These are often small, seemingly insignificant daily tasks that eventually compound and allow you to perform at a level that you previously never knew existed. This is a process that takes significant planning and progression, but the rewards are tremendous if you develop the self-discipline and toughness to follow through on the concepts covered in the chapter.

OUR MENTAL RESERVES

Research has shown that we have limited amounts of mental energy when it comes to making decisions in our life. In *The Happiness Advantage*, bestselling author and psychologist Shaun Achor explains that there is a key reason why we struggle to follow through on our intentions. As we move through our days, we are constantly faced with a barrage of situations where we must use our mental capacity to make decisions. The problem here is that we have only a set amount of mental energy, and once it is used up, we struggle to make decisions that we know are right. In these instances, we tend to fall back into our normal habits that lead us to counterproductive lifestyle decisions. This is something that I have experienced first hand working with people one-on-one and in group settings to create positive habits to transform their lives. Interestingly, it is small, subtle daily decisions in the moment that often lead individuals to situations down the road where they fall way short of their expectations. This happens even with people who have the best of intentions. The primary reason this is the case is because most people have not taken the time to understand the importance of habits and the consequences of relying solely on their mental capacities to make tough decisions.

One example that illustrates this point well and impacts a wide range of people is in the area of fitness. This exact situation is front and center at the start of the New Year when millions of people set lofty goals related to exercising and losing weight. These people's intentions are good, but they often fall short of their expectations because their approach is flawed and it eventually leads them back to a super cozy position on their couch. Are you curious as to why this is the case? Let's assume for a second that most people reading this book are not lazy at all. In fact, if you have read through the first 10 chapters, you are likely an ambitious individual who has a busy schedule each day. Yet, you probably find yourself failing to follow through on key activities that you know are essential to your success. If it is not a matter of being lazy, then why have you failed to follow through on a New Year's resolution that you are fully capable of accomplishing? The answer actually might be more empowering than you think.

When it comes to working out (and many other key initiatives), many people often make the mistake of waiting until the end of the day to follow through on their intentions. It often seems far more convenient to do it this way because you tell yourself that you will have more energy in the afternoon if you get more rest in the morning. Or you don't put the right structure in place to rise early and are forced to do it in the afternoon because you missed (or dismissed!) the alarm. Allow us to explore why this approach leads to an unsatisfactory outcome. Because working out is not yet a habit and normally takes self-discipline to implement, we immediately put ourselves at risk of not following through on our intentions by putting it off until later in the day. Remember the research on limited mental capacity we just mentioned? By the end of the day, we have often used up all of these mental reserves making decisions and our mind is worn out. As a result, we have the right intentions to improve our fitness levels, but we don't have the mental energy necessary to actually get ourselves off the couch and exercise.

THE IMPORTANCE OF HABITS

The point of the previous section is not to make you feel bad about instances where you have fallen short of expectations. The reality is that all of us do this in some capacity in our lives. If it is not exercising, then maybe it is eating better, reading for 30-minutes, or playing with your kids at the end of the day. The options are pretty much limitless depending on the things that are most important to you in your life. The point of bringing this up is to make you aware of situations we face and decisions we often make that rob us of the ability to live our dreams. By simply understanding research and how the brain works, we can adjust our approach so we have a structure in place that allows us to progress and succeed in key areas of our life. Given that we have a limited decision-making mental capacity, one of the keys to success is developing productive habits that occur naturally with very little effort. While the creation of habits can be challenging to establish, they are an essential success step because they will allow you to create a lifestyle that is necessary to earn the right to live your aspirations. We have already established the fact that you cannot rely solely on your mental capacity to make this happen. Instead, you must create a structure in your life that is conducive to following through on your intentions without using much of your mental reserves. First, let's discuss the concept of habits and how you can create ones that will transform your life.

WHAT EXACTLY ARE HABITS?

Habits are often defined as an acquired behavior pattern that is followed regularly until they become involuntary. When you consider this definition, it is easy to see that habits themselves can be either productive or unproductive in nature. When we fail to get up early each morning consistently to read, that becomes our habit and we often default to staying in bed to get more sleep. This would obviously be considered an unproductive habit. The same can be said for the previous exercise example where we fail to follow through on working out. Eventually this becomes our norm and these habits are more challenging to break because of our unproductive repetitions. On the positive side, it is always within your power to take action to replace these with productive habits that are conducive to success. Given the clutter all around us and our limited mental willpower, you must be proactive about putting a structure in place that will make it far more likely that you perform the right actions on a daily basis. By being consistent in the right daily initiatives, you can eventually create world-class habits that will take minimal mental energy to maintain. Easier said than done, right? While this is absolutely true, you can maximize your chances of this becoming a reality by making it simple to follow through on your intentions.

> It is within your power to create world-class habits that will take minimal mental energy to maintain.
> -@coytecooper

MAKE IT SIMPLE TO SUCCEED

We have all had situations where we fell short of our expectations. This is something that is germane to each of us regardless of our approach. However, when it comes to following through on our intentions, the reason we often fail to meet our standards is because we have not taken the time to set ourselves up for success. Even when you know the action items you must implement to make your goals a reality, there is a good chance that you will eventually stumble in your efforts if you don't put a structure in place that allows you to maximize efficiency in follow-through. In addition, there are simple decisions that you can make on a daily basis that give you the best chance of succeeding in your efforts. The key in this process lies in simplifying your approach so you follow through consistently on the action items that are most essential to realizing your goals and eventually living your dreams.

KEYS TO ESTABLISHING PRODUCTIVE HABITS

There is a reason why so many people in today's society struggle with developing productive habits. The primary culprit responsible for a lack of consistency in developing habits is laziness. Most people are simply not willing to put in the time and energy necessary to make them a reality. Given that you have ventured this far into the book, we will assume that this is not the case for you. It is far more likely that you now understand that living your best life is a challenging process and you are willing to make the investment. If this is an accurate description of your current mindset, then it is time to create a plan that will allow you to become a high performer. It is a process you must be willing to invest in on a daily basis over extended periods of time before you get a chance to reap the benefits.

> Most people are simply not willing to put in the time & energy necessary to make world-class habits a reality.
> -@coytecooper

1. PICK WORLD-CLASS HABITS. It seems like common sense, but the first step to creating a high performance lifestyle is choosing the right habits. No matter who you are, or where you would like to go in life, you must start by creating foundational habits that are conductive to success if you are going to achieve remarkable things. The most important part of this process is choosing behavioral patterns that allow you to progress towards your vision. If you are looking to advance in your career, it would make sense to cultivate a habit where you read the right books for 30-minutes each day. Given that the top CEOs in the world read an average of 60 books in a year, it would behoove you to carve out time to learn from the most effective people in the world via high quality literature. If you have determined that you need to improve the quality of your relationships, then focusing on listening better to others might be an area of focus for you. There are so many examples of habits you can strive to implement that will change the quality of your life. This book is scattered with productive ones that will allow you to progress towards your aspirations and to make your mark on the world. Pick some that make sense for your aspirations and get to work implementing them into your life.

2. LEARN FROM THE BEST OF THE BEST. If you are still unclear as to what habits you should initially pursue in your life, then take a look at people who are highly successful in your area of interest and see what makes them unique. If you are an aspiring entrepreneur and want to create an outstanding organization, then pick up *Delivering Happiness* by Tony Hsieh or *The Virgin Way* by Richard Branson and learn about how they succeeded in building some of the most creative companies in the world. It is possible this is not your interest at all and you simply want to become an inspiring educator who elevates the lives of students on a daily basis. If this is the case, then think about the teachers who impacted your life and visit them to learn about their teaching philosophy and approach. In the words of Jack Canfield, co-author of the Chicken Soup for the Soul series, "To change bad habits, we must study the habits of successful role models." The point is that there are always opportunities to learn from people who have achieved unique success in their lives. When you identify these people, study them to learn about the behaviors that allowed them to differentiate themselves from others. Once you learn these behaviors, it is simply about following through on making them a high priority part of your day so you can eventually make them a habit that allows you to progress towards your dreams.

> To change bad habits, we must study the habits of
> successful role models.
> -@Jackfield

244   COYTE COOPER, PH.D.

3. IMPLEMENT ONE HABIT AT A TIME. So, you have gotten to the point where you are excited about developing world-class habits and you know the ones that you want to implement in your life. It is time to make them all a reality immediately, right? Wrong. While it would be amazing to establish a variety of world-class habits all at one time, the reality is that they will each take time and their implementation often requires significant mental energy. Given that this is the case, the most effective route to cultivating outstanding habits is to focus on one at a time as you get started. This will ensure that you do not use up all of your energy reserves, which will in turn increase your chances of meeting your expectations. Equally important, this will allow you to narrow in on this habit and to learn exactly what it will take to follow through on your intentions. Once you learn to consistently follow through on the action item(s) that are essential to establishing your new habit, you can pursue another behavior that is essential to realizing your long-term vision. Eventually you will have a team of habits that will allow you to make a championship run.

4. BE PATIENT WITH YOUR PROGRESSION. As I have worked with people in the personal development process, it has become apparent that frustration often occurs when people have unrealistic expectations. When you set lofty standards for action items that are necessary to create a desirable habit, there will be times when you fall short of expectations. In the times when this occurs, it is important that you are patient with yourself and do not make it a big deal of your performance. While you should certainly never be excited about not meeting expectations, it is a part of the process and the most important thing is you learn from your situation so you can improve your efforts moving forward. This sounds familiar, right? It is essentially an extension of the "fail forward" philosophy we talked about in the previous chapter. Always acknowledge situations where you fall short of expectations and then

S INEVITABLE. PURSUE THE THING YOU ARE MEANT TO DO ALL OUT AND MAKING YOUR MARK IS INEVITABLE. PUR

move on to the lesson as quickly as possible so you can get back to making the habit a reality as soon as possible.

5. ALLOW TIME FOR HABITS TO TAKE HOLD. People in our society want instant gratification. We have already touched on this mentality earlier in the book. This is no different when most people approach trying to create a positive habit. They often get excited about a new behavior (e.g., eating better, exercising, journaling, reading) and the impact that it can have on their life, but they get frustrated after a week or two because they do not see tangible results in their life. This is the time when they claim that the strategies are not working and they fall back into behaviors that are much easier like sitting on the couch and watching television. Their lives do not change and it is because their expectations were unreasonable. When it comes to creating sound habits, research has shown that it takes a range of 21-66 days for a new behavior to take hold. So, if you want to get to the point where a behavior comes more naturally and does not drain your mental reserves, you will potentially have to work at it consistently for a little more than two months to ensure that it is a rock solid habit that will help guide you to success.

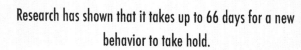

> Research has shown that it takes up to 66 days for a new behavior to take hold.
>
> -@coytecooper

TAKING THINGS TO A NEW LEVEL

If you have read this far into the book, then you are committed to taking your efforts to an entirely new level. My hope is that you are inspired to live each day so well that you leave a lasting impression on the people around you. When you are truly passionate about making your mark on the world, there will be a desire that drives you to create world-class habits that allow you to achieve mind-boggling things.

246 COYTE COOPER, PH.D.

There must be a pride about getting up each morning ready to do the things that other people are not willing to do to realize your goals. It is imperative that you develop a passion to persist at your most desirable behaviors until they become habits with the potential to transform your life with very little use of your mental energy. Once you establish these habits, you will naturally gravitate towards your aspirations while freeing up your mental capacities to pursue other high priority initiatives. In the meantime, start earning these habits by practicing some simple strategies that will enhance your efforts. You can start by learning to kiss a frog first thing every single morning. It probably sounds crazy to you now, but it will be a concept that will allow you to create outstanding habits that transform your life.

> You must have a pride about getting up each morning ready to do the things other people are not willing to do.
>
> —@coytecooper

KISS A FROG FIRST THING IN THE MORNING

In Brian Tracy's *Kiss That Frog*, he touches on simple, impactful steps you can take to maximize your chances at success in key areas of your life. Among them is a concept that he refers to as "kissing a frog first thing in the morning," which means taking your highest priority initiatives and doing them right when you wake up before you officially start your day. Rather than put them off, Tracy explains that you can build momentum when you take on the action items that are most important to achieving your goals. In addition, the process of doing them first thing in the morning ensures that you are not relying on mental energy later in the day to make them a reality. By performing these high priority tasks when your mental tank is full, you almost guarantee that you will follow through on these initiatives and eventually they will become a habit that reaps major rewards. First you must be willing to kiss that frog first thing in the morning though!

Eat a frog first thing in the morning and nothing worse will happen to you the rest of the day.
-@BrianTracy

LEARN TO WORK AT HIGH PRODUCTIVITY TIMES

While the morning is generally an ideal time to tackle your high priority tasks, this is sometimes not realistic because of your current lifestyle. It is also possible that you have learned from experience that you are a "night owl" and do your best work once everyone else is sound asleep. If either of these situations is the case for you, then adjust your schedule to place your high priority tasks in the times where you are personally most productive. However, before you make this decision, be sure that it is at a time where you can be consistent with your efforts. If it is at a time where distractions are more common or you anticipate situations that will demand your attention, then strongly consider these obstacles as you create your high performance schedule. It is definitely worth putting them at a time where you will be able to dedicate all of your energy to consistently following through on key initiatives. This is why the early riser option is so appealing. While there are certainly exceptions, this is a time where distractions are often low and work is easier to get done because it is quiet. Always remember that consistency is one of the keys to establishing world-class habits, and your ability to follow through on them with precision will determine your success.

SCHEDULE THINGS AT THE SAME TIME

Research has shown that consistency is an essential element when it comes to establishing habits. In addition to having to practice behaviors on a regular basis, studies have shown that habits often form more efficiently for people who carry them out at the same time each day. This is one of the reasons why the morning growth routine is so essential. By doing it at the same time each day, it allows your brain to adjust to the activities more quickly than when it is done at different times. So, if you want to be successful in creating world-class habits, learn to schedule your more desirable habits within a set time frame and be great at following through on a daily basis. Eventually the habit will take hold and the behaviors will become second nature for you.

Don't Overreact To Highs And Lows

In the time it takes to establish habits, it is inevitable that you will face times when things come easily and other times when they are extremely challenging. It is important you know this ahead of time so you can avoid overreacting to either one of these situations. On the one hand, life is meant to be challenging and there will be times when you really have to work at following through on your desired behaviors if you want them to turn into productive habits. In fact, there will likely be instances when you fall short of expectations because of the challenges that life presents. It is essential that you learn not to overreact to these situations. As we have already discussed, it is about focusing on the lesson in the circumstance you are facing and how you can improve your efforts in the future. However, this is not the only situation that you need to be aware of when you are trying to establish the right habits. On the flip side, there will be times when things come easily and your momentum allows you to breeze through the implementation of your behaviors with very little effort. This can often be the case when you first start a pursuit that you are excited about. While momentum is a good thing, it is important you do not make the mistake of overreacting to these situations. If you immediately respond to these situations and assume that things will always be easy, there will eventually come a time where you will be mistaken and frustration will emerge as momentum wears off and things get more challenging. The key is to make sure you use the momentum, but not to allow it to take you away from your central focus of developing world-class habits and earning the right to live your dreams. The best way to make this happen is to stay grounded and focused on the process so you can achieve remarkable consistency in your approach.

CREATE A HIGH PERFORMANCE CALENDAR

Even when you know the high priority behaviors you are planning to pursue and are inspired to turn them into a habit, you need to be careful about relying on your mental capacity to follow through on your intentions. This can even be the case when you are planning on working in high productivity times when your mental tank is full. The reality is there will be times when your brain overrules your intentions if you do not have the right structure in place. What is required to maximize your chances of success is a high performance calendar. This is a daily checklist calendar that includes your highest priority initiatives that are most essential for realizing your dreams and goals. In addition to helping you to organize your days from an efficiency standpoint, the structure also helps you to establish accountability that is necessary for developing world-class habits. If success is all about habits, then you need to do whatever is necessary to help you make them a reality. The high performance calendar provides stability in your approach, as it is a constant reminder when you fall short of expectations. It also serves another role that is more positive in nature. As you invest in positive repetitions, the high performance calendar will give you an overall picture of your progress because you will be constantly logging your results as you follow through each week. In addition to keeping you on track, this will also build momentum when you start to string together great days and weeks. It will serve as a constant reminder of the investments you are making and this will naturally allow you to build your confidence. If this sounds appealing, then get to work with the following steps to make your high performance calendar a reality.

STEP #1: IDENTIFY HIGH PRIORITY INITIATIVES. If you are going to create an effective high performance calendar, the first thing you need to do is to create an initial list of high priority initiatives that are essential to realizing your goals. The core foundation of this list should be habits that will eventually allow you to realize your vision when practiced over time. One great example of this would be the morning routine that includes reading the right books, journaling, and revisiting your goals. These would be considered foundational focus areas and will remain on your list because they are habits that will ensure you are always moving towards your full potential. We have touched on other examples that fall into this category as well throughout the book. With that being said, not all of your initiatives will fit this description. There will be others that will be unique to your one-year goals and that will be implemented on a week-by-week and month-by-month basis. For example, if your goal is to launch a new product effectively in the next year, you may have a monthly initiative to reach out to at least five new clients to tell them about the product each day. Once the product launches, this may change to something else depending on the priority of your goals. However, the premise of the high performance calendar will always stay the same, as it will look to identify key priority items where you can focus your time on a week-to-week basis.

STEP #2: PICK OUT YOUR TOP INITIATIVES. Not all high priority initiatives are created equal. While all of the initiatives you listed in the previous step are likely valuable, it is inevitable there will be select ones that will be far more essential when it comes to realizing your top goals. It is critical that you develop the ability to identify these peak priority initiatives so you know the first items to be included on your calendar. Given the limitations of the brain when establishing habits, it will be important for you to practice progression as you determine the initiatives to include on your initial high performance calendar. If you want to maximize your chances of success in your follow through, it makes the most sense from an efficiency standpoint to start with a few select essential initiatives that will receive your full attention. As you get comfortable with the schedule and show consistency in your follow through, you can look at adding initiatives that will allow you to improve your efforts. Always keep in mind that this is more of a marathon than a sprint and you must be able to follow through with investments over an extended period of time to truly reap the rewards that come with the establishment of world-class habits.

STEP #3: DETERMINE DAYS OF THE WEEK. It is not enough to simply choose the initiatives that you believe are essential to achieving your goals and dreams. Once you have performed this task, the next step is to determine the exact frequency of the initiatives so you can hold yourself accountable on a regular basis. For the purposes of this book, we will use days as the standard metric because they are the most common reference point for us to measure our progress. From an organizational standpoint, it makes sense to use weeks as our calendar format because it allows us to assess our progress within a digestible format. With this being the case, we must immediately identify the weekly frequency of our high priority initiatives (e.g., five times a week), and if less than daily, the exact days we will perform the tasks. It is important to be specific here because our ability to follow through will depend on the exact guidelines we set for ourselves. When there is less room for justification, we will always know the exact instances where we fall short of our standards. This also gives us tangible evidence of the periods when we are investing and progressing towards our goals. However, follow through is only one part of the equation as the quality of our investments also play a role in our ability to eventually earn the right to live our dreams.

STEP #4: INCLUDE RATING SYSTEM TO ASSESS PERFORMANCE. Living your best life involves a lot more than just going through the motions. This statement seems like common sense, right? Interestingly, this is exactly what most people do on a daily basis. They strive to do the minimum required to achieve success. When they learn about the importance of setting goals, these individuals write their goals down, but they spend only the required amount of time necessary to finish the activity. You know as well as I do that this will not result in extraordinary accomplishments. There is no question that identifying top priority goals and initiatives will immediately differentiate you from others who are not willing to take the time to do these things. However, once you have outlined these planning elements, you must learn to follow through on them exceptionally well on a regular basis to put yourself in unique company with other high performers. This is exactly why you must assess your performance on key priority areas on a weekly basis. At the end of your week, in addition to calculating the frequency of your follow through, you should rate how well you performed the task on a scale of 1 to 10 (with 1 being extremely poor and 10 being outstanding). This will give you an opportunity to constantly assess your performance so you know whether you are progressing towards your goals on a regular basis.

STEP #5: MAKE IT VISIBLE. Even when you have structure in place, it is still going to be difficult at times to follow through on your plans. You can drastically increase the chances of this occurring if you make your high performance calendar as visible as possible. If you use your computer on a regular basis, then make sure you have a copy that you can work from on the main device that you use. If you are not a technology person, then be sure it has a place at your desk or in an area that you frequently visit. While you certainly don't want it to dominate your entire day, the visibility will help tremendously with accountability as you get moving on your journey. In the times where you lack motivation, it will serve as a reminder of the things you must still get done to earn the right to live your dreams. You will find that this list will often make it far easier to follow through because it will make it extremely clear when you are falling short of expectations.

> The secret of getting ahead is getting started. The secret of getting started is breaking your complex, overwhelming tasks into small, manageable tasks, and then starting on the first one.
> - Mark Twain

Check, Please!

The premise of the high performance calendar is for you to identify simple, impactful daily tasks that will allow you to progress towards larger, more complex aspirations. The legendary American author Mark Twain had this to say about the process: "The secret of getting ahead is getting started. The secret of getting started is breaking your complex, overwhelming tasks into small, manageable tasks, and then starting on the first one." With your goals in place and your high priority action items now identified, it is time for you to get started. The high performance calendar should become your daily reminder of the exact things you need to get done to progress towards your full potential and vision. When you build up to a comprehensive list of desired behaviors and become outstanding at following through on them, you will be on your way to establishing world-class habits that allow you to achieve extraordinary things. This is what a high performance lifestyle is all about! It means you are doing the "little things" necessary each day consistently over time to perform at your highest level. There are few things more rewarding than when you know you are getting the most out of yourself. This is the exact time you will know you are earning the right to live your dreams and make your mark on the world.

RICHARD BRANSON

Today, Richard Branson is a billionaire who owns more than 400 companies and is the founder of the Virgin Group. He is recognized as one of the premier entrepreneurs in the world and has become known for his flashy approach to living and his ability to make things wildly fun. Interestingly, his rise to success did not come easily as he was dyslexic and dropped out of school at the age of 16. However, he did not let this stop him as he started his entrepreneurial career with the launch of a magazine called Student. From here, he continued his pursuit in the business realm when he founded Virgin Records where he went on to sign the Rolling Stones, the Sex Pistols, and Genesis. With all of his success, one of the things he has become well known for is his ability to focus sharply on top priority items. In fact, he once turned down over $500,000 for a single one-hour talk because he was not willing to dedicate his time to anything not related to his top three priorities. This is one of the primary reasons he has become one of the most prominent businessmen in the world and he has had a unique chance to impact millions of people through his efforts.

KEY SUMMARY POINTS

O   Success is all about choosing and implementing behaviors that will allow you to live an extraordinary life. When you are consistent with the right behaviors over extended periods of time (21-66 days), they eventually become world-class habits that will allow you to progress towards your aspirations.

O   When it comes to establishing sound habits, it is important to understand the initial limitations of our brain. We have a limited mental capacity dedicated to making challenging decisions so it is important to consider this when scheduling high priority initiatives.

O   It is essential that you schedule your most important tasks at high productivity times if you want to maximize your chances at success. Scheduling them first thing in the morning or when your mental reserves are highest is the best way to ensure that you follow through on your intentions.

O   The development of a high performance calendar can help you improve your level of focus and efficiency on a daily basis. When you are clear about your most important initiatives, this structure will help make sure you are accountable to your intentions as you strive to turn behaviors into habits that are conducive to success.

Chapter 12

Earn the Right to Live Your Dreams Each Day

 Some people want it to happen, some wish it would happen, others make it happen.

- Michael Jordan

Our society is obsessed with instant gratification. This has become the status quo expectation for a majority of the people in the United States today. At this point in the book, I don't need to give you a pep talk on not allowing yourself to settle for average in your approach. You already have a desire to be exceptional and that is why you are still reading and implementing the concepts in the book. You are striving to earn the right to live your dreams and that immediately makes you different than the millions of people who are looking for the easiest route to success. There are no shortcuts to meaningful accomplishments; you already know that. The key here is not to just have you comprehend this concept. It is time for you to cultivate a mentality where you take pride in making investments every single day to progress towards your aspirations. Other people will sleep in and make excuses for why they cannot get up. These same individuals will

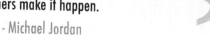

skip following through on their intentions because they don't feel like it. As a result, they will end up with unfulfilled promises and a life full of disappointment and regret. This is not for you though. I believe that you are ready to take responsibility for your life and to do whatever is necessary to reach your full potential. The only thing left to do now is get out and earn the right to live your best life!

TAKE FULL RESPONSIBILITY FOR YOUR LIFE

One of the first steps to earning the right to live your dreams is to take full responsibility for your life. This is a mandatory prerequisite for any extraordinary accomplishment you are pursuing because you must be willing to take full accountability for your situation in life to maximize growth and progress. If you have fallen short of expectations in the past, it is counterproductive to blame anyone other than yourself. Let's explore this from two potential angles that are common when assigning blame to someone else for your situation. First, there is the angle that someone else shortchanged you and this cost you an opportunity to advance in some desired way. It is possible that you are correct in your assessment, but it still does no good to take this route because you have chosen to dwell on something that you cannot control. In this instance, it would be far more productive to instead focus on how you can make the situation more desirable in the future. If you disagree, go ahead and assign blame and see where this gets you from a productivity standpoint.

There is a second angle to consider as well when you fail to take full responsibility for your current situation in life. When you get in the habit of blaming others for your circumstances, you are giving away the power that you have to control your own destiny. It is highly unlikely you will fully pursue your dreams and live outside of your comfort zone if you do not believe that you personally can make them happen. In addition, the moment you blame others for your lack of success, you are often letting yourself off the hook for areas where you did not perform to your full potential. Highly successful people learn to hold themselves accountable for their situation no matter what the circumstances are at the moment. Even if they are only one percent accountable for a negative outcome, they focus on improving that one percent so they can decrease the chances of the situation happening again. In short, they control what they can control and this allows them to live more efficiently than others. Lhamo Dondrub, the 14th Dalai Lama, explained this about accountability: "When you think everything is someone's fault, you will suffer a lot. When you realize that everything springs only from yourself, you will learn both peace and joy." The bottom line is you cannot blame other people for the lack of success in your life if you want the chance to achieve remarkable accomplishments. The moment you do this, you immediately give away the right to live your absolute best life.

NEVER SETTLE FOR LESS THAN FULL POTENTIAL

Another quintessential philosophy that is necessary to earn the right to live your dreams is being adamant about not settling for anything less than your full potential. Few have summed this pursuit up better than the legendary world leader Nelson Mandela when explaining, "There is no passion to be found in settling for a life that is less than the one you are capable of living." Everything we have covered in this book up to this point embraces this exact quote because the previous chapters have been designed to inspire you to raise your expectations for your life. If you are going to live an exceptional life, you must train your mind to constantly look for opportunities to improve personal performance levels. There is simply no room for average in this approach and you must resist all of the urges that come from your environment to settle for the status quo. So, how exactly do you earn the right to live your dreams? Well, you can start by striving to set extraordinary expectations that elevate you to a level that places you in the top tier of elite performers. Make it a general rule to never settle for anything less than remarkable when operating in areas of giftedness that align with your purpose. If your performance is not up to this expectation, then simply look for ways to improve until it meets your lofty standards. Earn the opportunity to make a lasting impression on the world by setting unique expectations that are considered "unreasonable" by normal standards.

> "There is no passion to be found in settling for a life that is less than the one you are capable of living.
> - Nelson Mandela

Everything Resides Outside Comfort Zone

At this point in the book, you already know that your success is going to depend on your tolerance to taking risks and failing forward on a daily basis. It is impossible to live your dreams, assuming they are lofty, if you are adamant about always doing what is comfortable. As explained by Robert Allen, co-author of the *One Minute Millionaire*, "Everything you want and more is just outside of your comfort zone." Did you get that? E-V-E-R-Y-T-H-I-N-G, as in every one of your dreams, is yours for the taking if you learn to push beyond normal expectations and make extraordinary your norm. Most people experience adversity and they immediately assume that it is a wall that was meant to show us our limitations. It is important to note that this is the mentality of "most" people who have settled for the status quo, and you are no longer a part of this group. It is perfectly within your power to completely reject this assumption. Highly successful people learn to see these situations as temporary roadblocks designed to test exactly how much you want something. They are the universe's filter to stop all of the people who are not serious about their dreams. Your job, then, is to bust through the wall so you have the opportunity to find an entirely new performance level in your efforts. Regardless of the circumstances you are facing, remind yourself to push a little more so you can become a part of a rare group who resides outside of their comfort zone. The massive dreams you have are meant to be achieved, but you must earn the right to live them by taking a path that few others are willing to take.

> Everything you want and more is just outside
> of your comfort zone.
> - Robert Allen

ALWAYS TAKE THE STAIRS

People who are looking for immediate success always seek out the path of least resistance. They are rarely willing to take the route where they have to earn success because they have been disillusioned by our society to think you can achieve great things with very little effort. Unfortunately, these individuals are misguided and they will eventually realize that there are no shortcuts to meaningful success. In the words of legendary author and speaker Zig Ziglar, "There is no elevator to success. You have to take the stairs." In other words, you must be willing to make daily investments over extended periods of time to have the confidence, connections, and skill sets required to live your dreams. The good news is that there are so few people willing to put in the work that there is never a line to take the stairs. This means that you can get moving on earning your dreams at pretty much any time. This real path to success is always open, but you must be willing to invest the time and energy to move up one step at a time. There will be times where you are so exhausted that you stumble down a few steps. In these times, you must get up, brush yourself off, and continue your journey. It will likely be a grueling process, but it will all be worth it when you take enough steps that you reach the top and get to enjoy the view.

> There is no elevator to success. You have to take the stairs.
> - Zig Ziglar

STEP WHEN YOU CAN'T SEE ENTIRE STAIRCASE

Once you have made the commitment to take the steps, there will be another obstacle that you will need to overcome in the journey to live your dreams. When it comes to vision, there will be times where your aspirations are so far away from your current reality that you will not know the exact steps necessary to reach your end destination. This is a normal part of the process as big dreams, when set properly, are by default way beyond our current means. It is not possible for you to close the gap in a short amount of time so you need to believe in your ability to achieve them one step at a time. In the words of legendary Civil Rights leader Martin Luther King Jr., "Faith is taking steps even when you can't see the whole staircase." It doesn't matter if you don't know every single step in your journey. Nobody does when they have lofty aspirations. The key is being willing to take steps when you are uncertain and then learning from the process. Eventually, your courage in this area will elevate your life and you will close the gap on your goals and dreams. However, first you must develop the ability to step regularly even when it is not comfortable to do so.

> Faith is taking steps even when you can't see the whole staircase.
> - Martin Luther King Jr.

THE ONLY CERTAINTY IN LIFE

The road to your dreams will be filled with uncertainty and that is something you are going to need to embrace. It is a mistake to think you must know the exact route you will take to realize your vision prior to taking action. Why exactly? There is no such thing as a 100 percent guarantee when it comes to pursuing your aspirations. It is like the myth of the boogey man. It simply does not exist. Well, that is unless you consider this one thing mentioned by former United States President John F. Kennedy: "The only unchangeable certainty is that nothing is unchangeable or certain." So, if you want to have an opportunity to live your dreams and make your mark on the world, you need to get used to being uncertain as you embark on your journey. Uncertainty will eventually result in clarity when you make the right kinds of repetitions often enough over extended periods of time. While we are on the topic of certainty, the one thing you can be sure of is that the best time to start moving on earning your dreams is as soon as possible.

> The only unchangeable certainty is that nothing is unchangeable or certain.
> - John F. Kennedy

THERE IS NO BETTER TIME

Are you ready to earn your dreams? The ability to answer an adamant "yes" to this question is the first step in making them a reality.

Once you are prepared to invest in the process necessary to earn success, the second question you must ask yourself is "when?" If you avoid this question, you will have a tendency to float in your efforts because you can always start tomorrow or next week. The problem with this approach is it almost always leads to another time that is not conducive to realizing your vision. In the words of author Holly Lisle, "If you have dreams you want to pursue, the time to pursue them is now. There is no perfect time, and there is no better time. There is only the time you lose while you are making excuses." If you want to earn the right to live your dreams, then get in the habit of taking action to make them a reality now. Today. Even if your actions are not perfect, the most valuable decision you can make is to get into motion so you can learn from repetition. Eventually, as others are waiting until tomorrow, you will differentiate yourself and take valuable steps towards your dreams. The key is to always learn to take steps today regardless of whether you feel like it or not. This is the one way to ensure that you are always moving towards your full potential.

> "If you have dreams you want to pursue, the time to pursue them is now. There is no perfect time, and there is no better time. There is only the time you lose while you are making excuses.
> - Holly Lisle

Earn It at All Times

While we are on the theme of time, we may as well discuss the importance of the frequency of your efforts when it comes to pursuing your dreams. We have made it crystal clear that you need to start and the best time to do that is right now. However, the actual starting line is only one part of the equation because you have an entire race to run if you are going to get the opportunity to realize your vision. It is essential that you cultivate a mindset where you are ready to earn it at all times. Anybody can do this when things are coming easily and momentum is high. When you feel like it, you will almost always follow through on your intentions because it is easy to do so. This is not what defines success. You earn the right to accomplish great things when your environment is not ideal. In the times where you are tired, frustrated, and/or don't feel like it, these are the exact moments where you differentiate yourself and earn the right to live your dreams. You must be willing to follow through on your key priorities at all times if you are going to make your mark on the world.

In Darren Hardy's *The Compound Effect*, he talks about the importance of capitalizing on the bookends of your day if you want to be successful. This refers to the ability to start your mornings on the right foot and then to be able to do some productive activities right before bed. The reason why the first bookend is so important is that it allows you to set the right tone for your mindset as you approach your day. When you place positive, proactive thoughts into your mind as you wake up, it provides you with a sense of clarity and focus that allows you to be far more efficient throughout the day. On the other hand, the end of the day is also a prominent growth time for a couple of key reasons. In addition to being a time where you can reflect and determine areas to focus on moving into your next day, it represents a time where you can take advantage of using the subconscious brain to your advantage. By investing in a single activity such as revisiting your goals right before bedtime, you can activate the power of this part of your brain so it gets to work on finding ways to make them happen while you are sleeping. It is important that you develop an ability to capitalize on all the minutes of your day if you want to live a truly remarkable life that impacts the people around you.

AT THE CRACK OF DAWN. The morning is a time where you truly have an opportunity to differentiate yourself from others. There are few people who are actually willing to get up early before the sun comes up to work on advancing towards their dreams. This means that you can differentiate yourself immediately from others by simply being willing to get up at 5:00am to do a morning growth routine. It is likely this will be challenging for you for the first couple of months, but then it will eventually become a habit and you will learn to love your quiet, productive time in the morning. The first step to earning the right to live your dreams is winning the "battle of the bed." Fight off the urge to hit the snooze alarm and instead get up and invest in yourself. This will be an investment that will pay huge dividends in your progression towards your vision and best life.

RIGHT BEFORE BEDTIME. It is inevitable that there will be times where you come home at the end of the day and don't feel like doing anything other than sitting on the couch and watching television. Similarly, as you approach the second bookend of your day, it is likely you will have moments where you are exhausted and just want to go right to sleep without performing high priority tasks like revisiting your goals. It won't even matter if the initiative only takes a few minutes because your mental reserves will be all used up and your self-discipline will be ready to call it a day. These are the exact moments where you need to revisit your high performance calendar so you can follow through on your intentions. In the times where you don't feel like it, and when others would simply give up, these are the exact times when you need to remind yourself to earn the right to live your dreams. Then follow through so you can capitalize on the power of your subconscious brain.

AT ALL OTHER TIMES. The morning and night periods are absolutely essential to your success. You should treat them as such as you plan your days from a growth and efficiency standpoint. However, it is also important to recognize that they only make up a small portion of your day from an overall time allocation standpoint. In between these points, you often have at least 12 hours that you must use efficiently if you want to be able to progress towards your aspirations. It is important that you earn the right to live your dreams by dedicating as much of this time as possible to your high performance calendar. The most challenging part will be learning to block out the clutter so you are able to dedicate your most precious time and energy to your high priority tasks. When you create the right structure and become great at following through on your intentions at all times, you will be well on your way to living your goals and eventually your dreams.

DON'T LET THE DAY OF WEEK DICTATE YOUR PACE

It likely goes without saying that you must learn to work on a regular daily basis if you want live a remarkable life that results in making a unique mark on the world. This certainly does not mean that you must work every single day because there is extreme value in making sure you take some days off so you can stay fresh. In addition, it should always be a top priority to spend quality time with your family and friends. With that being said, do not confuse this with a counterproductive approach where you are inconsistent with your repetitions. One of the biggest mistakes many people make is they allow the day of the week to dictate the pace of their approach. When Monday rolls around, they fail to make a productive transition back into the week and they spend their entire day disappointed that the weekend is over. This normally results in them wasting their entire day trying to get themselves back into a productivity mode. The same can be said about Friday when many people are counting the hours until the weekend. High performers who are passionate about their vision never allow the day of the week to dictate what they are able to accomplish. Instead, they capitalize on their weekly bookends and approach each day with a sharp focus on taking advantage of all the opportunities to progress towards their vision. They strategically build energy and momentum by consistently taking action on key high priority initiatives that are aligned with their goals. As a result, they often run laps around other people because they are taking full advantage of the time that has been allocated to them.

THE PROPER WAY TO BEHAVE

The legendary children's author Dr. Seuss had an interesting take on how to approach each day. Rather than settle for the status quo, he set out to be truly unique in his approach and had this mantra: "Today I shall behave, as if this is the day I will be remembered." Such a fascinating way of looking at life, right? It has a similar feel to the mantra of making each day a masterpiece, but in typical Dr. Seuss fashion, he just makes it sound a lot more intriguing. Oh, the places you will go if you will embrace this philosophy! Imagine the focus and energy we would have if we could take this advice and learn to live individual days to our full potential. We would be primed to take advantage of all of the opportunities around us that are aligned with our vision. To get started, simply follow the advice by Dr. Seuss and be amazing at living each day as if it is the day you will be remembered for. It will give you a sense of urgency that will allow you to pursue your passions with your full attention. In the times where you are proud of the way you lived at the end of your day, you will know you are on the right track to live a life that is truly worth remembering.

THE 10,000-HOUR RULE

One of the best ways that you can earn the right to live your dreams is by becoming an expert in the area(s) most essential to realizing your vision. If you want to establish yourself as a best-selling author, then it would behoove you to hone your craft until you are an amazing writer who can capture the attention of readers. So, how long does this take exactly? That is, if you want to become one of the best in your field? According to Malcolm Gladwell in *Outliers*, the high performers in a variety of fields dedicate an average of 10,000 hours specifically to honing their skill sets to reach their current level of expertise. In case you were wondering, this is the equivalent of nearly five years of 40-hour work weeks dedicated solely to a specific skill set. This is a remarkable demonstration of self-discipline that few are able to accomplish in their lifetime. If you want to put yourself in this rare group of high performers, then you will need to be willing to log the tremendous hours required to become an outlier. As you mull this decision, remind yourself of a general law when it comes to the pursuit of dreams: the bigger the aspirations, the bigger the amount of sacrifice required to make them a reality. Decide now if you are ready to make this type of commitment because it will determine whether or not you will get a chance to live your dreams and to make your mark on the world.

The Only Way To Excellence

Talent alone will never allow you to achieve extraordinary accomplishments. You will never be the best in your field if you are not willing to put in the time and energy necessary to earn it. This is a fact. The 10,000-hour rule applies to individuals in all fields and areas of interest regardless of an individual's skill sets. While talent certainly helps you excel, there is a limitation to how far you can advance if you are not willing to work towards your full potential. When you place a cap on your progression, it is inevitable that you will eventually get passed up because there will be someone out there willing to put in the time and energy necessary to master their craft. The key to excellence is getting up each day committed to reaching your full potential and progressing towards your vision. The inner desire to live your best life should be so strong that it dictates your lifestyle and the decisions you make on a daily basis. This starts with a willingness to practice your skill sets on a regular basis. Don't underestimate the importance of embracing failure because you must be willing to get out and learn from repetition to hone your skills to a level of mastery.

WE TALKIN' ABOUT PRACTICE

The term "we talkin' about practice" became infamous in the sports world in 2002 when Allen Iverson went on a rant in a press conference when being questioned about his preparation routine. Interestingly, he highlighted his tenacious drive to compete during games, but his message downplayed the importance of practice in his preparation to become a great player. It is as if Allen Iverson got temporary amnesia and forgot that practice, and the 10,000-hour rule, is exactly what allowed him to become a Hall of Fame type player. Following this press conference, it would have been wise for him to consider this impactful advice from bestselling author Malcolm Gladwell: "Practice isn't the thing you do once you're good. It's the thing you do that makes you good." This is the exact philosophy you need to embrace when you are striving to reach your full potential. Allow us to visit an example of an individual who achieved extraordinary accomplishments because of his willingness to put in the repetitions necessary to earn the right to live his dreams. He was obsessed with practicing because he knew that this was the one way he could maximize his potential during his college athletic career.

THE LEGEND OF "PSYCHO T"

If you follow college basketball closely, then you have likely heard the nickname "Psycho T." This is because this nickname belongs to one of the most accomplished college basketball players in the last 20 years. His personal accolades include (but are not limited to) four consensus All-American teams, four unanimous All Atlantic Coast Conference (ACC) teams, Wooden Award winner, and the 2008 National Player of the Year. He also helped lead the North Carolina Tar Heels to a National Championship in 2009 and went on to a career in the National Basketball Association (NBA). By now, you may already know that I am referring to Tyler Hansbrough. However, while his accomplishments are remarkable, his day-to-day approach is far more interesting for people who are looking to achieve success. While you may be thinking that pure talent is the catalyst for his success, his Hall of Fame coach Roy Williams has a different take on his accomplishments: "What Tyler has taught me is how much a young man can control through discipline and hard work. He's an example of someone who has gotten more out of what he's been given than anyone I've ever seen." When you study Tyler Hansbrough, you learn that what made him truly unique as a college athlete was his extraordinary willingness to put in extra repetitions to achieve his dreams. It was the 200 extra shots before every single practice that made him a four-time All-American and National Champion. These were the repetitions that allowed "Psycho T" to capitalize on the 10,000-hour rule so he could make his mark on the University of North Carolina and college basketball.

Do What Others Will Not

As Oprah Winfrey explained earlier in the book, there are no real secrets to success. If you are willing to put in the work, you can achieve the goals that you have for your life. However, if there is one thing you have learned from this chapter, it is that you must earn the right to live your dreams through discipline, focus, and hard work over extended periods of time. This is often far more difficult than it sounds and most people are simply not willing to sacrifice enough to achieve unique accomplishments. Geoffrey Colvin, the author of *Talent is Overrated*, explained this about the nature of success: "The reality that deliberate practice is hard can even be seen as good news. It means that most people won't do it. So your willingness to do it will distinguish you all the more." If you want to be an extraordinary performer and/ or human being, then you need to be willing to do things that other people are not willing to do. It is really simple at this point. You just need to flat out be willing to earn it. As you reflect on this chapter remind yourself that success happens one dream at a time, one goal at a time, one day at a time, one habit at a time, and one decision at a time. The time to capitalize and earn your best life is now!

THEODOR SEUSS GEISEL (DR. SEUSS)

If you have even an inkling of interest in children's books, then you likely know Theodor Seuss Geisel. Let me rephrase that. You are likely familiar with the name and workings of Dr. Seuss, who is a world-renowned children's author. Even if you consider yourself the biggest fan of his work, I bet there is something you may not have known about this amazing man's career. Did you know that Dr. Seuss had his first book rejected by 27 publishers? This alone would have been enough to make most people quit. But he was not like most people and he committed to earning the right to live his dream. Eventually his efforts paid off and he went on to publish classics such as *The Cat in the Hat*, *Green Eggs and Ham*, and *Oh, the Places You'll Go*! His books have sold over 600 million copies worldwide! Just imagine if Dr. Seuss would not have committed to persevering until he realized his vision. Hundreds of millions of children and adults would not have been able to enjoy his work, and the world would be far less creative. Dr. Seuss truly made a lasting impact on the world because of his willingness to continue to take steps when others would have quit.

KEY SUMMARY POINTS

O   If you are going to achieve remarkable accomplishments, you must first take full responsibility for your current situation in life. Regardless of the circumstances you are facing, you must seek out areas where you have fallen short of your full potential and immediately take steps to improve.

O   The ability to achieve success will depend entirely on your willingness to earn it. You must be willing to consistently take steps to progress towards your vision even when you are not certain how you will get there.

O   You earn the right to live your dreams by being willing to make investments when most people are not willing to. Earn it by intentionally capitalizing on the bookends of your days and by continuing to invest when other people are distracted. Commit to embracing the opportunity to progress towards your dreams every minute of your day.

O   If you want to be extraordinary at what you do, then be ready to practice every single day so you can hone your skills until they are at a level of mastery. Be ready to practice for years and years so you can capitalize on the 10,000-hour rule.

CHAPTER 13

STRIVE TO ASTOUND YOURSELF AND OTHERS

If we did all the things we are capable of, we would
literally astound ourselves.

- Thomas Edison

THE FINAL, CULMINATING step in this book is designed for all the
dreamers who are set on doing something unique to make their mark
on the world. Success is inevitable the moment you commit to doing
the little things consistently that most other people are not willing to
do. In other words, you immediately differentiate yourself the exact
second you commit to earning the right to live your dreams. When this
resonates with you, it is safe to say that you are not a part of the instant
gratification generation because you are ready to invest daily so you can
achieve all of your aspirations. You are ready to become a master of
living the fundamentals exceptionally well on a daily basis, and because
of this, you will eventually come to a point where your growth astounds
you. The interesting thing is that this moment will likely creep up on
you because you will not usually recognize your progress in the moment.
When it comes to single daily investments, you are often too close to

actually see the difference that it is making in your life. However, over time your investments will eventually compound and amazing things will start to happen in your life. This is when the outcomes will make your progress too obvious to miss. It is at this moment that you will be astonished by what you have accomplished and the person you have ultimately become as a result of your efforts.

ALL THE THINGS WE ARE CAPABLE OF...

The opening quote by the legendary entrepreneur and inventor Thomas Edison is one that you should put in a highly visible place so you see it every day. It is an ideal reminder of the untapped potential that lies dormant within every single one of us. If you could use all of your gifts to their full potential, you would accomplish things that would make a drastic impact on the world. The outcomes would be so truly remarkable that you would provide sound evidence that Edison is correct in his assessment, as you would literally astound yourself. This is a pursuit we should all strive to achieve at some point in our lives. We should all be so lucky as to be able to perform at such a high level that we get to experience this exact feeling. Make it one of your aspirations to live so well that you literally astound yourself because of the drastic impact you are able to make on people and the world.

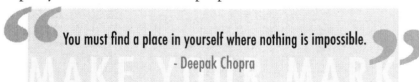

You must find a place in yourself where nothing is impossible.
- Deepak Chopra

IMPOSSIBLE IS NOTHING

If you want to get to a point where you astonish yourself because of everything you are able to achieve, then you must find a way to exterminate any limitations you place on your expectations. In the words of author and speaker Deepak Chopra, "You must find a place in yourself where nothing is impossible." Take a moment to process this statement. It makes sense, right? There should be nothing that stands in your way of pursuing excellence and your best life. It is essential that you train your mind to think that anything is possible when you are working within your area(s) of genius and are willing to earn the right to reach your full potential. You must get to the point where you simply do not believe in the word impossible. This is so important because there will be people around you who criticize you and tell you that your dreams are not reasonable. They may even have the nerve to tell you that they are impossible. Don't take it personally. In these moments, take a deep breath and remind yourself of this epic quote from one of the greatest athletes and boxers of all time Muhammad Ali: "Impossible is just a big word thrown around by small men who find it easier to live in the world they've been given than to explore the power they have to change it. Impossible is not a fact. It's an opinion. Impossible is not a declaration. It's a dare. Impossible is potential. Impossible is temporary. Impossible is nothing." This is your dare to go out and defy the odds. Astonish the people around you because of your extraordinary approach and ability to make a lasting impression on the world.

Anything's Possible Starts Somewhere

For many people, the "Impossible is Nothing" slogan is a distant concept because they have been taught to place limitations on their expectations. It is something that sounds nice in theory, but does not seem realistic in real life because of what our environment has trained us to believe. It is best to play it safe and settle for the status quo, remember? This is not for you though. You are at a point where every part of your being is urging you to go out and do something spectacular. The part you are wrestling with now is knowing exactly where to start. How do you go from a place of doubt to one where you fully believe that anything is possible? Anybody can give themselves a pep talk and get fired up in the moment to live their dreams. We have all done this at one time or another. It is an entirely different thing to sustain this feeling over time and firmly believe that you are capable of achieving remarkable things in the face of adversity and criticism. The question you now face is, "how do I make this a reality?"

The starting point in achieving remarkable things is simpler than you think. I guess it is a lot like many of the growth concepts presented in the book. The actual decision is easy to make, but the implementation takes self-discipline and follow through. In this instance, you simply need to make a steadfast decision that you want your life to stand for something special. My hope is that this is now an easy decision because you are inspired for an opportunity to reach your full potential. Once you have an inner desire to live your best life, the key is to not overwhelm yourself by thinking you need to accomplish everything at one time. Simply embrace the fundamentals and strive to be outstanding at cultivating world-class habits that are in alignment with your aspirations. Be proud of your ability to take action to realize your dreams every single day while others around you choose not to because they don't feel like it. In the times where you are a little uncertain and your vision is cloudy, remind yourself that all great accomplishments that our world has seen started somewhere small. Each of the legendary leaders who have impacted our society in an extraordinary manner has started with a single intention to live a unique life. You are no different in this regard. However, do not underestimate the importance of cultivating a strong inner desire to achieve remarkable things that make a drastic impact on the world in this process. You may not recognize it in the moment, but this is the point where you start your journey to replace the impossible that resides within you with a belief that anything is possible when you pursue something with your full potential.

Out With The Old, In With The New

It doesn't matter what your past has been. You can make a decision right now that your future will be drastically different. Listen, most of us have made the mistake of placing limitations on the things we can achieve at some point in our lives. It is time to replace this old used up scarcity mindset with a new one that focuses on abundance and possibility. If you are still fighting this concept, ask yourself a simple question: what do you have to lose by trying? Even for a pessimist, the worst-case scenario is that you try and end up back in your current situation doubting your ability to achieve great things. You might as well get out and see what you can accomplish when you pursue your full potential. When you replace limiting beliefs with uplifting possibilities, I would be willing to bet that you will eventually astonish yourself with what you are able to accomplish.

It's An Inside Job

It would be unrealistic to think you can instantly move from having regular feelings of doubt and insecurities to having full confidence in your abilities to achieve all your dreams. I would be setting you up for failure if I led you to believe that this was something you could accomplish in a short amount of time. While the process of change will start the moment you determine unequivocally that you want your life to stand for something special, there will also be a series of required investments you must make to pursue your dreams with full confidence. The key thing for you to understand is that confidence, and believing in your abilities, is an inside job. While you can absolutely receive structure and advice from others, the only way you can truly believe that anything is possible is by investing in yourself on a daily basis. When you have rocked your reps consistently over long periods of time, you will eventually come to a point where you truly believe that you can be remarkable. As you embark on your journey to live your best life, here are five ways that you can guarantee that you perform so well that you astonish yourself in the process.

FIVE WAYS TO GUARANTEE YOU ASTONISH YOURSELF

There is nothing accidental about living your best life. If you are not intentional with your efforts, it is unlikely that you will ever get to the point where you perform at such a high level that you astonish yourself. This is reserved for individuals who take consistent daily steps to perform at their highest level in their progression towards their aspirations. This will involve becoming world-class at implementing the unique aspects that have been covered throughout this book. However, there are an additional five strategies that you can implement to increase your chances of living your best life and astonishing yourself in the process as you make a lasting impression on the world.

1. FOCUS ON SIGNIFICANCE. If you want to truly astonish yourself, then the first thing you need to do is to focus on significance when establishing your aspirations. The best way to ensure that this occurs is by pursuing things that matter to you for all the right reasons. When your "why" is connected to your purpose, you will cultivate an energy that will drive your efforts on a daily basis. There are few things that can elevate your performance more than pursuing things that you are deeply passionate about. If you consistently chase goals and dreams that have significance, they will eventually lead you to a place where you are truly amazed by the person you have become in the process. If you don't believe me, then consider this insightful quote by legendary television personality Oprah Winfrey: "The key to realizing a dream is to focus not on success but significance - and then even the small steps and little victories along your path will take on greater meaning." When you choose the right pursuits for the right reasons, the journey will be truly remarkable and you will astonish yourself at what you are able to accomplish.

2. MAKE IT ABOUT OTHERS. One of the best ways to ensure that you stay inspired to live your best life is by making your aspirations about elevating others. There is nothing wrong with pursuing individual accolades and accomplishments, but be aware that they will only bring you a certain level of fulfillment because these initiatives will limit your ability to make a lasting impact on the world. The reality is that the most impactful legacies are the ones where visionary individuals find ways to influence people in a dramatic way. Author Kalu Ndukwe Kalu reinforced this concept when explaining this about legacy: "The things you do for yourself are gone when you are gone, but the things you do for others remains as your legacy." If you want to leave a legacy that is remembered long after you are gone from this earth, then make your vision about creating a better place for future generations of the human race. As explained by best selling author and motivational speaker Jim Rohn, "All good men and women must take responsibility to create legacies that will take the next generation to a level that we could only imagine." When you start to realize the impact that your actions can have on people, it will energize you to find new ways to improve your efforts on a daily basis. Tapping into this type of energy will inspire you to become better at influencing people so you can compound your efforts.

> The things you do for yourself are gone when you are gone, but the things you do for others remains as your legacy.
> - Kalu Ndukwe Kalu

3. DO WHAT YOU LOVE. Very few people get the opportunity to live to their full potential. Even fewer perform at such a high level that they astonish themselves because of what they were able to achieve. One of the primary reasons why this rarely occurs is because most people never do what it takes to live within their passion zone. In the words of American entrepreneur Malcolm Forbes, "The biggest mistake people make in life is not trying to make a living at doing what they enjoy most." If you want to perform at your highest level and make your mark on the world, you must find a way to do what you love as much as you can every single day. The one way to increase your chances of making this happen is by pursuing a career that is in direct alignment with your purpose and areas of genius. The energy and passion that come as a result will truly compound what you are able to achieve in key areas of your life.

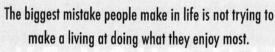

> The biggest mistake people make in life is not trying to make a living at doing what they enjoy most.
> - Malcolm Forbes

4. NEVER EVER THINK YOU HAVE ARRIVED. When you consistently invest strategically towards lofty aspirations, it is inevitable that you will experience success. This is a good thing and you should enjoy the fruits of your labor. However, you should never let your progress influence your approach by allowing success to go to your head. The key here is to commit to the philosophy that you have never arrived. This means staying level headed and not allowing yourself to get to a point where you believe you deserve to stop investing. If you experience tremendous growth and blow past your one-year goals, enjoy your success momentarily before setting new standards that take you further outside of your comfort zone. If your efforts compound and you are fortunate enough to realize your dreams earlier than expected, then seek out new aspirations that will inspire you to reach an entirely new level in your life. Never stop growing and pursuing your full potential. When you are constantly looking to improve the quality of what it is that you have to offer the world, there will always be a new challenge that you can pursue to maximize your potential.

5. MAKE A PROMISE TO PURSUE YOUR BEST LIFE. You will never be able to control the external environment in your life. Nor should you try to because it will only lead to frustration. However, the one thing that will always be in your control is your daily approach in the pursuit to reach full potential. Each morning, you can wake up with the intention of making each day a masterpiece as you strive to create world-class habits that allow you to progress towards your aspirations. In the times where you fall short of expectations, you can choose to focus on the positive and seek out ways to learn from the process of repetition. Make a promise to yourself to pursue your best life so you can achieve remarkable things. It is always within your power to strive to be the best you can possibly be, and this is something that no one can take from you if you are always focused on proactively living your best life. When this is your focus, it is only a matter of time until you are astonished by your progress and all the extraordinary things you are able to accomplish as a result.

RELEASE THE EMERGENCY BRAKE

When it comes to dreaming big and pursuing lofty aspirations, the mistake that most people make is they hold back and place limitations on their expectations. This can even be something subtle such as a small doubt where you question your abilities. While it is not a major thing, it is enough to slow you down because you are focusing on negative thoughts that impact your progression. It creates a tension that you must battle against in your progression to realize your aspirations. This would be similar to jumping into your car for a long trip to a desired destination with your emergency brake on. This tension, while it will not completely stop your movement, is enough to significantly slow progress while also draining your gas tank. As a result, your trip takes way longer than you expected and you end up frustrated because it feels like you will never reach your end destination. The same is true for people who constantly doubt their ability to reach their aspirations. If you want to reach your full potential and live your dreams, then you need to learn to release this emergency brake so you can break free in your pursuit. Eliminate your limiting beliefs so you can focus your full attention on progressing as efficiently as possible towards your dreams.

The Time Is Always Right

When it comes pursuing your best life, there is no better time than now to commit to a structure that will allow you to reach your full potential. This is the right thing to do because you have been blessed with one-of-a-kind gifts that you are obligated to use to make the world a better place. As explained by the legendary civil rights leader Martin Luther King Jr., "The time is always right to do what is right." You can and should make a decision right now for your life to stand for something that will be remembered beyond your time on this earth. Stand for something that inspires the people around you to live a better life. Stand for vision. Stand for excellence. Stand for self-discipline. Stand for consistent daily investments. Stand for earning it. Stand for all of the things that will allow you to make your mark on the world.

> The time is always right to do what is right.
> - Martin Luther King Jr.

ONE STONE CREATES MANY RIPPLES

It is not your job to go out and instantly change the world with one single act. This is not a reasonable expectation. It is also a mistake to think that you will make your mark on the world all by yourself. Mother Teresa, one of the most impressive human beings to ever grace this planet, explained this about her pursuit to make an impact: "I alone cannot change the world, but I can cast a stone across the waters and create many ripples." One single stone and many ripples. It seems like such a simple concept that you can't help but question its legitimacy when it comes to making a lasting impact. Yet this is exactly what you need to do if you want to make your mark on the world. Do not be confused by Mother Teresa's quote because her individual actions did change the world in a drastic way. However, it was her ability to impact people and to get them on board with her mission that allowed her to create millions of ripples that still cascade today all across the world. But the single, consistent daily acts are what made this a reality. You will be no different than Mother Teresa in this regard. Once you live your life to full potential and perform at your highest level, you will have an opportunity to influence the people around you. If you grow to the point where you cultivate a skill set that allows you to add value to people, this is when you will start to cast stones that will make many ripples. Do this often enough and you will eventually get a chance to make your mark on the world.

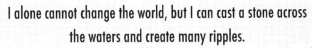

I alone cannot change the world, but I can cast a stone across the waters and create many ripples.
- Mother Teresa

PREPARE FOR YOUR FINEST HOUR

When you follow the principles outlined in this book and live your best life over an extended period of time, there will come a moment where you have an opportunity to use your areas of genius to achieve something truly remarkable. Former British Prime Minister Winston Churchill explained this about our unique opportunity: "To each there comes in their lifetime a special moment when they are figuratively tapped on the shoulder and offered the chance to do a very special thing, unique to them and fitted to their talents. What a tragedy if that moment finds them unprepared or unqualified for that which could have been their finest hour." You now have the initial steps necessary to make sure that you are fully prepared for your finest hour. Now it is time to get to work so you capitalize on the opportunity to do something unique to make the world a drastically better place.

I Believe In You!

I truly believe that you are ready to take your life to an entirely new level. How do I know this? The fact that you have reached this point in the book means that you are different than most other people. You are in the small minority of people who actually read an entire book that they purchased and this makes you different. While this certainly doesn't guarantee success, it does mean that you know how to follow through on your intentions. The reason that you are still reading is because deep down you know that you have the potential to do something remarkable with your life. It might be a small urge at this point, but make no mistake, there is a desire somewhere deep within you to do something to make the world a better place. Now you just need to add a little fuel to this spark so you can turn it into a full-blown fire. It is time to start the journey to live your absolute best life! I believe that you are ready to cast a stone. I believe you are ready to make ripples. I believe you are ready to be the butterfly that causes an enormous storm. I believe you are ready to realize your full potential.

Because of all of this, I believe you are now ready to go out and earn the right to make your mark on the world. You get one chance to live this life so be intentional each day about making it remarkable and memorable!

THE MAKE YOUR MARK MASTER

YOU!

This page is dedicated to you, the reader. If you made it to this point in the book, then you are different. You now have everything you need to get started building an extraordinary life full of passion, energy, and abundance. It is time for you to go out and create YOUR own story. I truly hope you will create one so unique that you make a lasting impression on the world. Once you do, we would love to hear about your journey at **www. TheMakeYourMarkBook.com**. We will be featuring the most unique stories on my *Earn the Right to Live Your Dreams* podcast and in one of my future books so please come share your accomplishments with us. Let's work together to create a #MakeYourMark movement that makes the world a much cooler place!

YOUR TIME,
YOUR STORY,
YOUR LEGACY,
MAKE YOUR MARK

WILL YOU HELP ME HAND IT FORWARD
AND
MAKE YOUR MARK?

If you enjoyed *Make Your Mark* and it has impacted your life in some way, will you share it with people who have the potential to go out and achieve cool things while making the world a better place? You can gift them a copy on Amazon or simply give them your copy.

In order to help the book gain momentum, it would be awesome if you would post about it on social media recommending it to others. I will be highlighting the best book pictures from readers on social media and on the website so please tag me when posting them (Facebook **Coyte Cooper – Make Your Mark**, Instagram *@coytecooper*, and Twitter *@coytecooper*). There will be prizes handed out consistently to the best social media shout outs so please post often as you read the book!

In addition to recommending the book to others, it is really helpful to have positive reviews on Amazon. I would be extremely grateful if you took a moment to write a review.

Finally, if you truly want to maximize your chances of achieving great things and making your mark on the world, be sure to move through the complementary Mastermind Course using the access code at the start of the book.

Now go out and make your mark on the world! It's your time!

Sincerely,

ACKNOWLEDGEMENTS

Anyone who has written a book knows how much time and energy it takes to do it right. I am so blessed to have an amazing wife Brandy who supported me throughout the process and who has always encouraged me in the pursuit of my (and our) dreams. I am also grateful for my two awesome little kids, Carter "The Cube" and Mya "Yemma," who inspire me daily without even knowing it.

This book is dedicated to my parents, Gene and Lisa Cooper, because there is no one who has made a bigger mark on my life than them. They have always put me first and I have learned so much about being a great human being from them. I cannot possibly ever repay them for everything they have done for me, but I hope this book will show them how much they mean to me.

I would also like to thank my brother Matt for all of his support while writing this book. I will never do an acknowledgements section of a book I write without mentioning him because he is one of my best friends on the planet.

When I think about people who have made their mark on my life, there is no person that has influenced me more outside of my family than my former high school coach Ron Bessemer. To this day, I am so grateful for the lessons that I learned from him, and many of these are scattered throughout the book.

In terms of creating the book, there are some people who really stepped up to make it special. Jennifer Deese did an amazing job with the cover and interior design and was an integral part of making the book unique.

I was blown away by her unique gift to see things differently and am so glad she was a part of the publishing process.

I would also like to express my gratitude to my launch team for this book. Scott Grant, Mark Facciani, Sam Ferguson, Josh Nolan, Natalie Rene, and Eric Rossitch stepped up big time to make this book special and I am so thankful for their efforts and friendship.

There are so many people who have influenced this book by making their mark on my life throughout the years. While I cannot possibly mention everyone here, please know how much I appreciate the impact you have made on my life.

ABOUT THE AUTHOR

Dr. Coyte Cooper is an author, coach, and speaker committed to helping people perform to their full potential so they can achieve extraordinary things. Passionate about helping people realize their highest aspirations, Dr. Cooper uses his past experience as an NCAA All-American athlete to help people understand exactly what it takes to perform at a high level each day.

He is the author of *Impressions: The Power of Personal Branding in Living an Extraordinary Life*, the host of the *Earn the Right to Live Your Dreams* podcast, and the creator of the *Fundamentals of High Performance* course. He is also the founder of Make Your Mark Enterprises, which is committed to helping leaders and organizations perform to their absolute full potential. He earned his Doctorate in Sport Marketing & Management from Indiana University—Bloomington in 2007. He currently resides in Noblesville, IN with his wife Brandy and his two kids Carter and Mya.

FOLLOW
DR. COOPER

COYTE COOPER - MAKE YOUR MARK

@COYTECOOPER

@COYTECOOPER

COYTECOOPER

GET OUT AND

MAKE YOUR MARK

IN BUSINESS, COMPETITION, AND LIFE.

Take advantage of custom life
and performance training.

Dr. Cooper has created unique training opportunities that are designed to help you perform to your full potential so you can create a life you absolutely love. Let him show you how to go out and achieve great things so you can make your mark on the world.

> ➢   One-on-one coaching

> ➢   Speaking and keynotes

> ➢   Online courses

> ➢   Workshops and retreats

> ➢   Live events

Learn more about opportunities at
www.CoyteCooper.com

coytecooper@gmail.com

Made in the USA
Lexington, KY
02 October 2016